G000136899

You're Being Ridiculous!

The Fun and the Frenzy of Fostering

C.E.A. Forster

Published by C.E.A Forster
www.ceaforster.com

British Library Cataloguing-in-Publication Data
A catalogue record for this book is available from the British Library.

ISBN: 978-1-9999858-0-6

Cover design by bespokebookcovers.com

Formatting by lornasvoice.com

To Mum, Dad and to my boys, with all my love.

Biography

C. E. A. Forster, is a pen name and an anagram of Foster Care. The purpose of my writing with a pen name, as I hope you can appreciate, is to protect not just my identity but the identities of all the children I have cared for and will refer to. The book is factual, but all names have been changed.

I live in the UK. Aside from fostering, I live a fairly normal life. I go out to work, I pay a mortgage, I do all the fun but sometimes mundane things that most of us do day in day out. I never would have imagined that I could have written a book and I suspect that this is a one off so please just enjoy it.

This book was originally written for my own benefit, so that in my old age I would never forget the love and the laughter that being a foster carer has brought to me. I simply want to share it with you.

www.ceaforster.com
@cea_forster

Contents

Chapter 1

Introduction and a Welcome to My World

"Claire!". Then the voice from the trampoline at the end of the garden becomes slightly louder and more insistent, "Claire!". He knows he's not meant to shout to me from the garden when I'm busy indoors and yet still the bouncing and yelling continues, "Claire!", with an elongation of my name that only a frustrated six year old can manage. It quickly turns to a "Mum" bounce "Mum" ... until I relent with a pang of guilt at this choice of word and go to the back door, where I quietly yell back "You know you're not meant to shout at me from the trampoline". Yes, you can quietly yell. It takes practice brought on usually by a feeling of parental or, in my case, carer humiliation but it can be done. It's loud enough that he hears you but low, growly and hoarse enough that he knows he's in the wrong and also you hope no one else hears you chastise him. Still, at the top of his voice and at his full height of bounce he shouts with all the volume he can find "But Claire, it's important", bounce, "we just need to know", bounce,..."what grows first" bounce, "your penis or your balls?"....bounce.

Now be honest, do you actually know the answer to this question? Well, if you do, given the time on your hands right now to consider it, then you're more informed than I was. I say this because while I had a fair idea of the answer, I wasn't factually sure enough to

2

corroborate it in a voice loud enough for my foster children to hear me at the end of a 40 foot garden, and without feeling that I was alerting my neighbours to the inadequacies of my pre-pubescent anatomical understanding. I raced to the trampoline, hands dripping with dirty dishwater, my face grimacing with a mixture of laughter, embarrassment and mortification and said as firmly and as sweetly as I could muster "Can you please not shout from the end of the garden, the neighbours do not want to hear your questions". "So, what's the answer?" Neil asked innocently as he and his older brother Owen stood looking at me through the safety netting where they were seemingly trapped until they had the required information. "Well", I said in a whisper, concerned that the birds or the bees might hear me, "I think it's your penis, because you're born with that and you don't really get balls until you're a bit older; now if you're finished on the trampoline you can go inside, we'll Google it and then you can get ready for your bath".

This event, a verbatim account, should probably fall somewhere in the middle of my story, but I will go back to the very beginning now and lead you through the trials, tribulations and sheer joy of my time so far as a foster carer.

You will know what foster care is, Google it if you don't, and you can appreciate that the majority of what happens is confidential, so names are of course altered. For those who know me personally I will be easily identifiable as these are stories well told and told well to friends and family. I have been a foster carer for just a few years now. I'm a single carer; not single through choice but my Mr Right just hasn't found me yet. I consider myself to be a fairly normal forty something year old although some might dispute this. I work full time, I had a dog called Ross who has since died and was soon replaced with another called Bailey and I have no children of my own. Put simply, I felt that rather than me add to the population of the world, I would prefer to look after and nurture those already born. I have absolutely no idea where this desire to care comes from but I find it the most rewarding experience and want nothing more than to share some of it with you.

This book was never intended as a memoir, biography or even a training or warning aid to potential foster carers. The initial purpose in my writing this was so that one day when I'm old and grey, a long way off yet, I will be able to read, recall and chuckle at these events. I started out with a big long list of occurrences, that then became this cathartic process of writing and the result is this book and my simply wanting to relay to you the funnier side to fostering.

You're Being Ridiculous!

Kids are kids, they should be allowed to be kids and without burden. I feel privileged to be a foster carer and children really are the most precious beings that any of us can get to know and love, but my goodness it can be testing.

Chapter 2
Rookie Carer

I was at work on a Friday afternoon when I got the phone call from social services that I had been waiting for but also dreading. I was a rookie foster carer, I had been through the lengthy fostering acceptance process to prove my solvency and sanity and was approved as a carer long before this first call came in. A pleading social worker asked me to take two brothers aged seven & six, Owen and Neil. I knew nothing about them or their background but took the bull by the horns and agreed that

I would take them; I mean, how hard could it be and after all, this is what I was wanting to do, wasn't it?

On the drive home from work it occurs to me that I'm not as prepared as I could have been. The beds are made up and ready but do I have toys or games for little boys? Do I have food in the house? What will they eat? What will they be like? All these unknowns are whirring through my head and then within minutes of arriving home the bell rings and my beautiful, single, care free life disappears in the time it takes me to unlock and open the door.

How had I allowed myself to imagine that these children would be likely to be shy, timid, nervous or quiet? I think someone had alluded to this in the various training sessions I had previously undertaken. I, or they, couldn't have been more wrong and I could do nothing but observe in disbelief as these two boys burst into my home, with barely a hello, and proceeded to race through the house bouncing off the walls and the furniture like Tiggers on Speed! Their social worker Elizabeth came in, the boys were gone, unstoppable and still tearing through the house, upstairs, downstairs and out into the garden. They went up the garden fence, up into the apple tree where they swung for a few minutes, violently kicking at each other and eventually falling into a crumpled heap onto the grass below, rolling around like a couple of lion cubs. I hope you can forgive me the animal comparisons but it's the only way I have of describing this particular introduction. Ross the dog had sensibly positioned himself, upright and alert but safe on his bed; his whole body appeared to be quivering and all I could give him was a consoling pat and a polite request to please stay where he was and I would see to him later. He willingly obliged and cleverly decided that starvation and loneliness was a safer and better option.

As Owen and Neil scampered and fought in the garden, Elizabeth gave me some more detailed information on the boys and their circumstances. I assumed this was intended as bedtime reading, although I was doubtful at this point that there would ever be a bedtime for them or me. The swinging monkeys, lion cubs, hyperactive tigers, whatever you want to imagine them as, were now back inside and ready to say hello, but only on the condition that they were given a drink and something to eat. Elizabeth, with a slightly pitying look in her eye, checked I was ready to be left alone, said her goodbyes and that she would be in touch on Monday.

I closed the door on a desperate-to-depart social worker and thought, now what? What do I do? Feed them? Talk to them? When I returned to the kitchen, Neil was standing on the table with his shoes still on, hitting the ceiling light and making it swing so it felt like I was in a nightclub with strobe lights. Owen was in the sitting room taking his clothes off muttering that he was hot and didn't want to wear his school uniform anymore; he raced back into the kitchen seemingly quite happy in his pants and wondering what was for tea.

Fish fingers, beans and mashed potato was the answer to my immediate problems and to their empty growling tummies. In the fifteen minutes that it took me to throw this culinary delight together, I had persuaded Neil to get down off the table and to take off his shoes but not his clothes, and I had tried unsuccessfully to cajole Owen into putting on some other clothes that I had found for him; he seemingly preferred to remain in his pants but had for some reason decided to put his socks back on. As the potatoes boiled, the fish fingers cremated and the beans stuck to the pan, we assembled at the kitchen table in varying states of dress and undress to eat our hearty meal. At this precise moment I was just pleased that for the few seconds their mouths were full and they couldn't speak I was able to think and formulate my plan of attack; or should I refer to it as their new boundaries and imminent early bedtime routine. Although relatively silent, apart from grunts and squeals, with food in their mouths they still found the ability to kick one another under the table and I found myself intrigued at their co-ordination of food to mouth while constantly kicking each other. I've since tried this and it's not as easy as it sounds; you're definitely at risk of placing a fork intended for your mouth into your eye. With clean plates from all three of us there was a demand for pudding...damn it, I thought to myself, as I don't have anything apart from a couple of out of date yoghurts which is fine for me but I can't be responsible for poisoning them on their first night. We settled on bananas and custard with one liking just banana and the other giving meaningful death stares at this prospect but content with just custard. I had both banana and custard to prove a point, although I'm not sure what point I was proving whilst not feeling in the least bit hungry. As one chomped and the other slurped it brought me another couple of minutes silence to continue with my master plan of getting them to bed. I had a horrific feeling in the pit of my stomach that it simply wasn't going to be achievable; I couldn't envisage either of them ever not moving or screeching. I've known, encountered, babysat and looked after many children over the years but these two brothers seemed to have appeared from a planet unknown to Earth and mankind.

At this point they had been in my home for less than an hour and already I had heard more inane chatter, hysterical laughter and bickering than I had ever thought imaginable but it was now or never for Mission Calm Down and getting them to bed.

Actually it wasn't too disastrous to begin with thanks to my babysitter, otherwise known as the TV. I wish I could say that the boys sat still and watched The Simpsons, their choice, but as I left them alone in the sitting room to race upstairs and run the bath for them, I could instantly hear the shrieks from downstairs. Not a lot of TV was being watched as I arrived back in the sitting room to find them on the floor, with Owen sitting on Neil's head, and the beans we had just had for our tea evidently proving his digestive system was in fine form. I got them both up off the floor and while Neil was unsurprisingly a little upset but unhurt, not to mention his very green pallor, we headed upstairs for them to have a bath. Thankfully for me, they excitedly jumped in together like two little seal pups, declaring that they had never had a bath before.

That comment in itself was shocking to me. I couldn't imagine getting to the age of seven and never having had a bath. I suspect they may have showered in the past but I've often wondered if in fact they hadn't and that this was why during their time with me they seemed to like being out in the rain so much. I suddenly felt a sadness for them, tinged with a feeling of guilt that I have a memory of the fun, warmth and security that this simple pleasure gave me in my childhood. Through the humour that I write with and the happiness that all of the children I will refer to have given me, let's not forget their very real and genuine states of trauma and neglect. I am not wanting this to be about the suffering that these kids have experienced, as that would not make for pleasant reading, but let's please just bear in mind through this book that their behaviours and their entire little beings are a result of their previous environments. I can't and won't write of some of the awful, heart wrenching circumstances that the children in my care have been through, the failed contacts with birth parents, the disappointments of promised occasions, their feelings of rejection or inadequacy. Neither will I write of where they have gone to when they have left me but I feel it's important to share that while they can be hurt or even irreparably damaged when they arrive, with the right love, care and security, they can leave in a much happier place, brimming with confidence and, depending on the length of their stay, with little pieces of me. They learn love, laughter, fairness and resilience, all of which I can only hope they will retain, even in part, as they go through childhood and on into adult life.

Chapter 3
Pee Wars

So, once Neil's tears had been dried and his pride restored following his near death gassing experience the first bath was unimaginably complicated. I very quickly realised that I needed to explain the dangers of water to a six and a seven year old and this came as a bit of a surprise to me. They moved as much and as quickly in the confines of a bath as they had done in the garden and if I couldn't stop them or calm them down then there was going to be an accident. I'm really not being melodramatic, they were both in unknown territory and they had no concept of the potential risks of drowning one another, or perhaps they were aware and I needed it to stop. As I feared for their safety and my own, this was the moment where I found within me a previously unknown dictator, also possibly not from this planet, and where the rules began. No standing, jumping or diving in the bath. No swapping ends, no holding your brother's head under the water to see what he looks like when he is dead.... things like that. My first problem was that if I spoke it to them nicely, they wouldn't even hear me. If I raised my voice slightly and gave a tone that suggested, "listen to me this is important and I want you to do what I ask", they still wouldn't hear me. If I spoke really firmly and loudly and asked them to stop what they were doing immediately, they would hear me, look at me as if I was a bit batty and not quite making myself clear to them, and there was still no change to proceedings. I am reluctantly admitting this as surely no parent or carer should actually shout. We know that we should speak calmly to our children so that they can understand our reasoning and that they need to have the chance to have us understand their point of view.....well guess what, that's just ridiculous! If I really shouted at the top of my voice and stared them right in the eye giving a simple one word instruction, like "Stop" or "No" or "Enough" or "Out", with no explanation whatsoever, they beamed at me and did what was asked of them. These little people responded happily to my guilt-ridden dictatorial commands. So, "Stop" and Neil stopped dancing in the bath, Owen knew "No" meant not to drown his brother for his own entertainment, they both knew I had had "Enough" and that it was soon going to be time to get "Out".

You're Being Ridiculous!

The problem of course with these two children is that they both want to be first at everything, or last, depending on what it was that they were doing or being asked to do. I am well aware that this is perfectly normal sibling rivalry, I'm quite sure that I was like this with my siblings, but this was extreme, it was exaggerated, it was constant and it was absolutely exhausting. It was literally never ending and with no sense of rationale. Ridiculous in fact, a word that I came to use repeatedly over the next few months. You're being ridiculous!

They both wanted to have their hair washed first, so to avoid an issue and to try to just get the job done, I found an ability to wash and rinse both heads of hair one handed and ambidextrously. I didn't even know this was possible and I certainly didn't know I was capable of it. Neither wanted to be first out of the bath and both wanted to be last. So I tried in vain to get them to come to an agreement that one would be first out tonight and the other would be first out tomorrow night. It sounded a sensible enough compromise to me and I felt this was a good solution but I sat in the bathroom on the toilet seat with a towel looking at these two immovable objects both of which refused to be first tonight. I was pondering which one would be easiest to haul out first. Neil, the younger one, you would assume would be lighter and easier but he appeared to be so wriggly and covered from head to toe in bubbles and Owen the older seemed sturdy, cross legged and welded to the bottom of the bath. Do I leave them there until it gets so cold they can't stand to be in freezing water or is that considered child cruelty? I was pretty sure by now that they would have staying power and I wasn't really wanting to sit there waiting for them to make their own decision; we could all be there for hours.

Reasoning certainly hadn't worked and was seemingly an alien concept to them. I finally suggested they both get out at exactly the same time and dry themselves but neither wanted to be the first to touch the floor. After much co-ordination and balancing precariously on the edge of the bath they both thankfully touched down safely onto the bathroom mat and at exactly the same time. Drying didn't happen on this occasion and was unimportant to them although it didn't take many more baths for them to realise that being wrapped cosy in a towel made the whole bath time experience much more enjoyable. They were both off out of the room before the bath had even emptied, and I had already pulled the plug out in my attempts to get them to move. Their eventual disembarkation from bath to bedroom had taken all of twenty seconds. I had put pyjamas on their beds and after shaking the water and bubbles from their bodies, they got excitedly into these while still wet. That was the least of my worries. Everything was done so quickly, at tornado speed, and I didn't have time to wonder if their quickness would subside and in fact I found myself, usually slow and ambling, propelled by their speed and haste.

To my delight, and I'm very easily pleased by now, I remembered I had stocked up on new toothbrushes in preparation for my first arrival. I began to consider that it was either luck that these toothbrushes had probably been a two for one offer or had I had some sort of a sadistic premonition of there being two of them? They brushed their teeth, hopping, dancing and jigging from foot to foot which reminded me that next I needed them to go to the toilet before getting into bed. How any child can hop, talk, punch, laugh and brush is beyond me and needless to say it wasn't the most effective brushing of their teeth but I suspect it was the closest they had been to any plaque removal or fluoride in a long time, if ever. I found myself in the doorway of the bathroom hopping and jigging with them; their nervous excitement apparently contagious to a normally calm and placid person. Once they had spat vigorously and mostly into the basin I suggested they go to the toilet before getting into bed. I left the bathroom, still jigging and hopping quickly, as I had pre-empted the next row about who would go first or last but I didn't yet have an answer for resolving it. I don't mind admitting that leaving them alone in the bathroom to work this out for themselves was a serious rookie error.

Have you ever heard of pee wars or is this a game that only these two brothers had created and learnt to play? Having closed the door, in order to give them some privacy to pee, I then heard the most alarming squealing and hysterical laughter interspersed with communications such as "I declare war, are you ready?" "Go...go down, go up a bit, gotcha, aaaaghh that's gross!" I could never have imagined or perhaps naively have foreseen the carnage that could be caused by spending a penny before bedtime. Let me explain. Pee wars, is apparently where they both pee at the same time and they have to connect streams before it hits the water at the bottom of the toilet bowl. I can tell you without any shadow of a doubt that the force and velocity at which they peed caused urine to be dripping from the ceiling, down the mirror, down the walls and down everything other than what it should have been dripping down. I burst into the bathroom to witness this devastation but they looked so happy and cherubic and I simply couldn't speak. I channelled every word, thought or action I had into my own now neurotic jigging, beamed at them as if this were all perfectly normal and when they were out I unashamedly closed the bathroom door figuring it would dry and could be cleaned up at a later date when I had returned from the asylum.

Next came the squabble over who had which bed, and needless to say they each wanted the bed that the other wanted even if one or both changed their minds at varying points of the decision making. Actually, a bed with a mattress raised off the floor was a novelty to them; I soon realised that pretty much everything I had once taken for granted was a new experience for them and that they just simply didn't know how to act or what to expect next from this new environment. This decision of who goes in which bed wasn't being made by standing calmly discussing pros and cons, it was being decided with Ninja kicks as they flew through the air at each other jumping from bed to bed. So, out came my inner dictator again – "Neil this is your bed and

You're Being Ridiculous!

Owen this is yours. There's no debating or discussing it, just get in" and in they got, good as gold and without any arguments. Well that was easy, I'm getting the hang of this raising my voice now and rightly or wrongly it had the desired affect. Bed time stories were selected, by me, as neither could decide what story they would like and if they had decided then they either wanted it first or last which became too ridiculous for me to even consider a compromise. What surprised me enormously by this point was how attentively they listened to the stories and how very quickly these roguish, lively little boys became quiet, softer and engaged, with their heads, at first resistant but gradually resting on my newly ambidextrous shoulders, and not a sign or sound of any of us hopping. The end of the second bedtime story came and I could see and feel their heightened excitability, nervousness, whatever it was, re-emerging and so I swiftly stood up and said firmly & loudly "Right, it's eight o'clock, I'm going to turn out the light now, it's time for you to go to sleep. If you don't sleep you won't grow and I want you to grow taller and to be clever. I don't want to hear a peep out of you until the morning and unless you need the toilet you stay in your beds and under no circumstances do you come downstairs". Wow! A long speech I know but they were actually listening to me, this is progress. I gave them each a kiss goodnight, assured them everything would be okay, turned out the light, pulled the door to but not quite closed and stood for a second at the top of the stairs, waiting for the convulsion of giggles. It never came. The last I heard was Neil saying earnestly to Owen "we had better go straight to sleep" and Owen replying "okay, I don't want to be a dumb dwarf!".

Now, I know this is not a politically correct statement but I am just writing it as it happened and out of the mouths of babes. I don't believe there was any offensive intent and quite honestly I felt guiltily responsible for having put the idea into their heads that they wouldn't grow without sleep. I decided that as it was quiet and they had heeded my pleas for silence and sleep I would cover the details and repercussions of this at a later date. I crept downstairs, into the kitchen and slumped in a chair at the table. As I sat with my head in my hands, the dog courageously crept towards me, resting his head on my leg with a plea to be fed, albeit three hours late.

I sat and sat, waiting I'm not sure what for? Had they silently smothered each other? Had they jumped from the first floor window in a bid for freedom? After only half an hour, curiosity and concern got the better of me and I crept back up the stairs. I listened carefully, not a sound, and just to check my fears weren't true, I quietly opened the door to find both absolutely sound asleep and still in their designated beds. I felt a wave of relief that day one, all three hours of it, had been a success and my two little lion cubs were sleeping peacefully.

The evening was now my own again. My first night of foster care and although I was still feeling a sense of heightened anxiety I also felt I had achieved something that only a few hours ago had seemed highly improbable; they were in bed and actually sleeping. I gave myself a mental pat on the back; hadn't I done well! I settled down to watch TV but unable to concentrate, due to my continued nervous jigging and hopping trepidation, I phoned the ones who had bathed me, read me bed time stories and who were now my sounding board for venting my worries; my mum and dad. We all have them or had them. Some of us may know them, some may not, some may have a good relationship, some may not; that's life but

You're Being Ridiculous!

I've been lucky and I'm not ashamed to admit it. Mine have unwittingly and possibly regretfully made me into the person I am today and so they can surely help bear the brunt of this path that I have chosen to take.

As I relayed to my mum the events of the evening, I don't think I mentioned the pee wars as I had somehow blocked this from my mind, the call then had to be ended abruptly as I could hear a crying out from the bedroom. It was about ten o'clock and I raced upstairs to find Owen up out of his bed, crying and dripping wet. At first I thought he'd had an accident and wet himself but it became apparent that he'd suffered a night terror. With a swift change into a fresh pair of pants and a T-shirt (I wasn't yet prepared with multiple pairs of pyjamas) he went straight back to bed and out like a light. This sadly continued every night for several months but he and I both learnt to deal with it quickly and calmly and he always claimed never to have any recollection of these moments. I will never know what caused these night terrors for him or if it will ever fully resolve itself but we both dealt with it and by the time he left me they had lessened significantly and, dare I say it, had almost stopped.

I got myself to bed soon after this and I would love to say that I was able to sleep soundly as I usually do, but sleep evaded me this night as I lay worrying about what tomorrow would bring and whether or not I was capable of keeping these dangerously lively boys alive until Monday.

Chapter 4
Counting the Cocoa Pops

Neil woke at about six in the morning and although I wasn't properly asleep I only became aware of this alien figure at my bedside staring at me when I rolled over to check the time. I got out of my bed and sat on the edge blinking back the tiredness. It dawned on me as I came to that he's only just six and without his brother to goad him on he was looking a little lost and vulnerable. The loving part of me gave him the quick cuddle that he was quite obviously wanting but then the mean, early morning miserable part of me told him it was far too early to get up and that he needed to go back to his bed. Start as you mean to go on was my new motto for surviving. I'm pretty sure he didn't go back to sleep but he was calm, seemingly happy and most importantly to me the hopping, the jigging, the speed and the haste of these very busy boys hadn't yet begun.

Up to now, the only reason I would ever have got up before seven o'clock on a Saturday morning was if my house was on fire and even then I'm not sure I'd wake. Those days are gone and I have to remind myself that this change to my life is my choice and I need to get over it, get up and get on. I have two dancing, prancing boys in my room, clambering over and under my bed, swinging from the bed posts. This is the moment that I realise that I won't be seeing anyone I would like to see swinging from my bedposts again for the foreseeable future. If I ever felt I was missing a man in my life then really, what chance was I going to have of finding someone prepared to put up with this noise and level of activity so early in the morning. Again, I silently repeat to myself – this is your choice, get up and get on.

We all clambered downstairs in our pyjamas, Owen in his pants and T-shirt with no mention of the previous night's events. Neil instantly asked if I thought he had grown but thankfully there was no mention of dwarfism and so this issue of helping them to understand the rights and wrongs and equalities of the world could wait for another time. It did however start the marking of heights on the kitchen door and over the months and years ahead watching their own growth became an important part of their time with me. Tragic as it may seem, I have decorated my kitchen more than twice in the last few years and have been unable to paint over these markings. Perhaps one day they will return to see how little they once were and for me to see how much they've grown.

I was feeling relatively calm but our first breakfast was as eventful as I had feared. The lion cubs were desperate for food and punching, poking and kicking at one another they looked as if they might start to actually eat each other if they weren't fed soon.

Now I come back to their need to be either first or last, left or right; this would over the coming days, weeks and months involve up and down too. Who would sleep in which bed, the left or the right? Who would sit in which chair at the table? Who would sit in which car seat? Who would get their cereal first? Does he have more Cocoa Pops than me? Who goes up the stairs first? Who goes up the stairs last? Who comes down first? Who goes through the door first? Who goes through the door last? Who cares?! This has to stop or I will be committed!

You're Being Ridiculous!

Exasperated before the day has even begun, out comes my inner, and now fairly permanently outer, dictator although I prefer to think of it as my authoritativeness. I decided there and then to pick my battles carefully and to declare my own variation on pee wars. I established instantly who sat where and told them categorically that this was going to be the same for every meal and was never going to change until they learnt not to argue about it. There! Mission One completed, and they sat in their respective seats with their little legs kicking at each other under the table. Keeping them in their chairs was proving impossible, no matter what distractions I tried to put forward for them in the two minutes it would take me to get their cereal. I gave up trying and rather despairingly just let them kick each other while hoping that any bruising would be minimal. I was working on the basis that the quicker they started eating the quicker peace and quiet would resume albeit just for a brief period. As soon as I had placed the bowls of Cocoa Pops, the only cereal I had bought for the initial arrival of a child, in front of them they started at it with their paws, sorry, I should say hands; you need to understand that this all happened many years ago and writing it and recalling it is bringing back the feeling of panic that was enveloping me at this time. With mouths stuffed full of Cocoa Pops and before I had made it to the fridge and back for milk, it took all of two seconds for one of them to say "he's got more than me" and for the other to retort "no, he's got more than me". These statements weren't just made as one offs, they escalated quickly into full blown rows, tantrums and physical fighting. I sat as calmly as I could with my bowl of Bran Flakes, poured the milk into my own bowl and said "Enough! Okay, well both of you can count out your Cocoa pops and whoever has more can then divide them equally between you". Owen looked at me as if I was barking mad, which I believe I was on the verge of being, and Neil solemnly started to count but stopped when he realised he couldn't get past ten. There was a moment of silence where neither one of them knew quite what to say or do next; I had an opportunity to pour their milk, as equally as I could manage without actually resorting, as was suggested by Owen, to a measuring jug.

Now, the plan for the day, as had been loosely formulated during my inability to sleep, was as follows –

Wash and dry their school clothes. Do a food shop and somehow make it exciting by allowing them to pick some things for themselves. Take the dog for a walk. Buy them pants, socks and a few items of clothing each. Buy them each a pair of trainers and replace their holey school shoes and if there's time later in the afternoon then we can go to the park or play football or do something fun or anything that will tire them out.

This was my plan and while I'm aware that children and shopping is never a great combination I had little choice as all these things had to be done and it's just them and I. The load of washing was put on, I suggested we all went upstairs to get dressed and of course the histrionics began again for the race to be first up the stairs or was it last, I can't remember. Well, the race was on, and stupidly and stuck in the moment I found myself stampeding over two little boys to ensure that I got to the stairs and up them first. Fortunately there were no injuries to either of them but hurt pride and a look of shock on their faces that I could have done such a thing. I hadn't moved so fast in years and found myself momentarily embarrassed at my own childishness as I danced at the top of the stairs and chanted "I was first, I was first!". With all of us in their bedroom, I had battled to be first through the bedroom door too, I found them both some trousers, kindly donated to me by friends who knew that I would need them someday, a T-shirt each and some kind of sweater or hoodie. They were dressed, I wasn't and so the issue arose again of how to do this while leaving them alone for five minutes. In case you've wondered about whether or not I have showered myself, I can tell you that the answer is no. Is this bothering me? Yes, it really is, but honestly, what can I do? At this moment my hygiene, and my sanity for that matter, didn't feature; the boys were simply not safe to be left to their own devices so I was going to have to work this out later in the day. I plonked them in front of the babysitter again, hoping that this time he or she might be rather more captivating, and sure enough this allowed me a comfortable five minutes in between advert breaks to get dressed, squirt on some deodorant and perfume to mask the whiff of rookie carer.

The dog, shut in the kitchen so that the boys didn't savage him or vice-versa, was fed and let out into the garden for a few minutes while I gathered myself and them into the car. Right on cue the bickering started again. Who was going to sit in which car seat, the blue or the grey and which side were they going to sit on with their respective chairs if indeed they could make that choice without killing each other first; I'm not sure they could have agreed on this either? The car seats, blue or grey and position, left or right wasn't so easily resolved and as I tried to bundle them into the car in the hope that they may just sort it out for themselves there was a full on fight and no amount of one word yells from me of stop, no or don't was going to change this. Both boys lying on the back seat had to be hauled out of the car by their flailing arms and legs. I knew by now of my ambidextrousness but I didn't really know my own strength. I had caught hold of a limb of each of them, bodies still attached, as I pulled them out of the car and dropped them onto the driveway. Now what do I do? What are they going to do? I couldn't think quickly enough but then they made it easy for me. Without warning, and I certainly didn't see it coming, they both launched at me laughing loudly saying "do that again Claire, do that again, that was so funny. Please, please do it again". Well ha bloody ha! It's not funny and I'm furious with you, I thought to myself, but their laughter was infectious and I don't quite know how but we all ended up rolling around on the ground; me, an exhausted rookie carer and my lion cubs. I proceeded to spend the next twenty minutes throwing these boys around the garden on a freezing January morning, laying the very early foundations of what was to eventually become the most adoring love all round.

Chapter 5
Pants, Shoes and Frozen Peas

We piled into the car, seating issues temporarily resolved by the Dictator, and we set off to get them some clothes and shoes. I was only really wanting to get the essentials and to get in and out of these shops as quickly as possible. We went first to Matalan but once out of the car, their speed, carelessness and disregard for their own safety or that of others was a sight to behold. My one word yells were not sufficient in this environment not to mention embarrassing for me, as they were definitely, or defiantly, not hearing me while everyone else was.

I walked briskly into the shop, with a developing hop and a skip, to try to get near enough to one of them to make a grab, but to no avail. I last saw Owen disappearing through a rack of ladies dresses and I last saw Neil heading for the changing rooms at the back of the shop. I felt I needed my dog with me to round them up. I couldn't catch one of them either physically or by their attention and so I stood no chance of getting them both. I had no option but to plough on through the shop, with a backward glance and a quiet yell of "I'm going to get you some pants" and I hoped that they would follow. I set off, determined that they needed pants and socks and that this was what they were going to get. They had actually disappeared. At this point I was slightly panic stricken, feeling out of my depth and wondering what on earth had made me think this fostering malarkey was going to be a good idea but I made the choice to move on regardless, in the hope that someone else would round them up and return them to me. By now I was beyond caring what other people thought of them, me or my parenting skills. Actually, what was also going through my head was that I needed to make my purchases as quickly as possible and get outside the shop before they did and be ready to pounce as they came through the automatic doors.

I browsed for all of two seconds, got their pants, socks and another pair of pyjamas each and was in the queue for the tills when a lady appeared holding Neil by the arm. I was surprised to find myself irked that she wasn't tenderly holding his hand, and judging by the look on her face she would have gladly held him by the scruff of the neck. He pointed to me from across the room and I was even more alarmed to find myself happy to see him and actually quite pleased that after less than 24 hours he could identify me in a line up. The nice lady muttered something about the changing rooms and how I really shouldn't leave a child unattended. I smiled sweetly, apologised profusely, all the while thinking I would like to ask her advice on how I could ensure that an escaped child wasn't unattended. I suddenly realised Owen was still missing and I stupidly called after her "there's another one still missing so if you find him can you return him too?". I don't think she can have heard me but to my shame the others in the queue had heard and I'm sure there was a chorus of disapproving tutting!

I had Neil firmly, not tenderly, by the hand and as I was called to the next free till, I was aware that Neil had seen Owen. I was busy paying and while entering my pin number with one hand I re-established an even firmer grip on Neil's wriggling hand with the other. I felt if

You're Being Ridiculous!

I had one of them with me then the other would never want to be far away. When I had finished paying and we walked towards the exit the relief I felt was enormous at seeing that Owen was safe. The fact that he was happily doing what I can only describe as a Bruce Forsyth pose with sunglasses and a pair of boxer shorts on his head almost seemed irrelevant. In that moment I just felt pleased that they and everyone else in the vicinity were unharmed and that I had achieved my objective of pants and socks. Owen reluctantly left behind the pants and sunglasses he had chosen and we moved on to find a shoe shop but not without me ensuring that I had a boy and a shopping bag in the one hand and a boy and my handbag in the other. Check! All was as it should be and we three briskly walked, with a slight skip and a hop, to the ever increasing chorus of queue tutters!

The shoe shopping was almost a pleasant experience by comparison and I was even able to release my hold on them. They seemed fascinated by having their feet measured and with new sizes of shoes required we set off to the relevant sections to get a pair of shoes each for school and a pair of trainers each. They were fairly calm and sensible with their selections and made no fuss if I said something was too expensive. I paid and we left and went back to the car; they jumped into their designated seats without any squabbling. It was still only eleven in the morning and I thought perhaps, just perhaps, my day was going to get better.

We arrived at Aldi to do the food shop. I had them both by the hand from the second they were out of the car and neither of them liked it but they knew why. They wriggled and writhed to get free and, wondering how I was going to push a trolley and hold both of their hands, I opted to give a stern word to them before entering the shop. They listened and they heard me say that I wanted them to stay right beside me at all times, that they could pick their own cereal and if they did this and if they were really good then we would do something fun in the afternoon. With hindsight I should have thought of the fact that Aldi usually stock their cereals immediately as you enter and so the chances of them being kept engaged in the shopping process were going to be minimal.

They selected their separate cereals with careful consideration and then once the packs were in the trolley things started to get a little tricky. I had asked them to each hold a side of the trolley, this was also argued about as to who would hold the left or the right, but this made us too wide for the aisles and it was quite blatantly inconvenient to other shoppers. Every second I was preventing an attempted escape from one or other or both of them. I didn't know how I was going to be able to let go of the trolley for the two seconds required to pick up my chosen items while also keeping an eye on their movement and bid for freedom. As a distraction, I was going to ask each of them alternately to grab the things I was wanting, my inner dictator had to decide on who went first with this particular job, and then it happened. I met a friend of mine and in the time it took for us to simply say hello, the boys were gone.

With cheetah-like speed they were at the end of an aisle skidding on their knees before I could even open my mouth to yell quietly. Out of sight now, I explained quickly to this friend that Owen and Neil had very much arrived and I was having an absolute nightmare of a day. All she could do was laugh at me, I like to think in a friendly kind of way, but when we both heard the clatter of trolleys, the angry voices saying "slow down" and the squeaking new trainers and giggles coming from afar she agreed that I perhaps needed to get on. I reached the end of the aisle, hurrying passed all the fruit and vegetables that I was hoping to buy but having already made the decision that this shopping trip was simply not going to work. Could we survive the weekend on cereal, milk, bread, eggs, yoghurts and fish fingers and whatever tins I have in the cupboard? Yes, we were going to have to. I did a supermarket sweep that Dale Winton would have been proud of, albeit just for six items but in a record speed I'm sure.

Now the hunt was on for Owen and Neil. I stopped in my tracks, listened hard and yes, I heard it. No, I didn't hear the boys' laughter or squeaky trainers, but I heard a new slightly more melodic chorus of tutters! I strolled towards the harmonious sound coming from around the frozen peas and found myself trying to pretend to the gathering crowd that I was a shopper just like them and that I wasn't the person responsible for these children who I still couldn't see. Then I saw them or at least I saw Owen and I saw a choir of tutterers congregating around him and the frozen peas but where was Neil?

The movement in the freezer chest under the panes of glass, crawling from one end of frozen sweet corn to the other end of frozen peas, caught my eye. The horror and disgust on several shoppers faces was enough to make me consider turning around and leaving these unattended children but I couldn't be sure that Owen would actually let Neil out. Never having had one I can't be sure, but I think I was as close to having some kind of a panic attack as I have ever been before or since. I battled through the bystanders to reach the freezer only to see Neil's face and hands pressed up against the glass grinning from ear to ear. He was beaming with delight and the glass was quickly misting over with the heat from his breath. I slid open the glass against Owen's protestation, hauled Neil out, grabbed a bag of frozen peas as if to make the point to the choir that this is what I had asked him to get and that he must just have fallen in.

I marched them to the tills, the pair of them with not a care in the world and no idea of the embarrassment they had caused me, and the titter of tutterers sounding like a bad case of tinnitus ringing in my ears. As I queued to pay, I reluctantly accepted that I currently had absolutely no control over them. I asked them to wait for me at the packing ledge and wasn't in the least surprised to hear the laughter first and then to see two little commando-style bodies slithering along the ledge at some pace and heading straight towards each other for an intended big collision. It's time to get my little worms out of here! I didn't return to this Aldi for over 4 years; I couldn't face it and in the years that Owen and Neil were with me I never took them shopping for food again. I did feed them of course, but shopped during my lunch breaks at work and while they were safely in school.

Chapter 6
The Padded Cell

Arriving home to find Ross delighted as ever to see me gave me a renewed vigour for getting through the day. The boys re-explored the garden and seemed content to be running around while I unpacked my meagre shopping and made them a jam sandwich for their lunch. I called them in and we sat, again in our designated seats, and ate. The under-the-table kicking continued but I ignored it and they looked visibly relieved that I was ignoring them as they quite simply couldn't help themselves and my constantly asking them to stop wasn't helping anyone. Lunch was almost enjoyable, with a lot of laughter, chatter and the first real opportunity to just sit with them and with no need to be anywhere.

We took Ross out for a quick ball throw, the weather was awful and the way the day was panning out I had decided that a long walk with a neurotic dog and two lively boys was not going to be my idea of fun. It may have been useful from a tiring them all out point of view, but to be honest I was exhausted without the walk and I had come up with an alternative plan for them.

I was in a slight quandary, as I had said before shopping in Aldi that if they behaved I would do something fun with them in the afternoon. Under normal circumstances, given their behaviour, I would absolutely stick to my guns and refuse to do anything but they weren't even aware they had done anything wrong and I had reached the point of needing to care for my own sanity and not just Owen and Neil's well being. A soft play centre was the answer to all my problems. It was inside, they couldn't escape, we would all remain dry, they could run around for hours on end and exhaust themselves and I could sit in the café area for hours on end; perfect. The boys were beside themselves with excitement and it was lovely to see. It was genuine excitement and not the sort of forced hilarity that it had been before. We set off in the car again, with a request by Owen to swap seats but this was not agreed with by Neil and so the squabbling began again. I suggested they were both being ridiculous and they were instructed to remain in their designated seats which one did happily and the other reluctantly.

We arrived at the soft play centre, all animosity regarding seat swapping forgotten. They got out of the car sensibly, not flinging the doors open into adjacent cars as they had done in the morning. (My sincere apologies to car owners in the area where I live.) We three walked nicely, hand in hand, through the car park, a little excited hop and skip from both boys and a relatively normal amble from me. Perhaps, just perhaps, this would be OK and we could all have some fun. They can have fun bashing themselves against padded walls and I can have fun with a cup of coffee and without the need to watch the chaos but in the full knowledge that they can't get out or come to harm. I should confess that I knew at this point that other children could still come to harm and were in fact in great danger but somehow this didn't seem to matter. I just needed some time to stop, think and prepare for how I was going to get to the end of the day.

We went in, I paid, we put their shoes in the shoe rack, I took off their jumpers and off they went. As I released them I had the most enormous sense of relief that I didn't have to see or hear them for at least, hopefully, five minutes. Then of course I felt guilty, they're children after all, children that are scared and hurting inside. I needed to remind myself of this, get a grip, and reinstate my usual compassion. A cup of coffee would help and so I went to the counter, unaware of where either of them were, and got myself a coffee and some squash for them if they were to ever return. I found a table with a view of the padded monstrosity before me and wondered if this is perhaps what it felt like to need or appreciate a padded cell. Would people stare if I was to pop around the corner and bang my head repeatedly against the side of this thing? I suspect they would and so I took my seat, sat back and tried to relax. I actually really did relax. From time to time I could see them running through and round this padded thing, kicking soft footballs at each other, sliding down inflatable slides with all the normal hilarity you would expect from two little boys. Yes! This seemed pretty normal and I was relaxed.

We had been there for a little over half an hour when they remembered I existed or at least they were thirsty and they hoped I might be able to help. They had some of the squash and they had a packet of crisps each – for all you healthy eaters out there, I know this isn't ideal but seriously this was just day two. Quite frankly the trauma of the morning and the fact that we weren't going to be able to eat much this weekend due to the scarcity of food in my house meant I had to feed them something. Don't forget this wasn't now about good foster care, this was about keeping me and them safe and alive.

Some more time went by and I was reading someone's discarded newspaper when the silence was broken but not by my child or children or at least I didn't think so. First of all, this child was screaming "Mum" from way inside the padded cells and so why would it occur to me that it's one of mine? I'm not sure they had even called me by my name at this point and so I certainly wouldn't have expected Mum. Not to mention the fact that as a foster carer you're meant to discourage them from calling you Mum – there must be a very good reason for that but I have to confess that I often can't follow the Mumbo Jumbo guidebooks of foster care.

The screaming of 'Mum! Mum!' continued and I glanced up out of nosiness if nothing else to see who's child it was. I caught myself as I was about to tut at a parent that could leave a wailing child. The wailing child was getting closer and obviously finding their way out of the padding. Still yelling, and not yelling quietly, for their Mum, the cries were getting more and more exasperated. I remember thinking, surely you would recognise your own child's distress but no one was moving. We were all subtly or not so subtly looking around at each other to see who it was that was unable to identify their upset child.

Well, you will know fine by now that of course it was my child, only he's not my child, is he, and I had never heard him cry before but what happened next snapped me out of my relaxed state and propelled me back into my new world of utter helplessness. Neil came out from the middle of the padded cell, with real tears rolling down his beautiful little face, his arm and finger held high in the air. He was making a beeline for me and already I could see the looks of disapproval that it had been me that was neglectful in hearing my child's cries. He was still quite a way from me and just as I was about to stand and go to him he yelled, and I mean really yelled at the top of his voice, "some fat f***ing bitch just sat on my f***ing finger!". Ground, swallow me up.....now! Oh my goodness, not only am I a bad mother, except I'm not a mother, but I must also be potty mouthed for my child to even know such words, let alone to be able to put them in the right context. I momentarily started wondering if perhaps he was incredibly bright to be able to speak so eloquently at such a young age and then I came back to reality. Should I go to him, now only metres from me? Should I yell at him for using such revolting language? Should I stand on my chair and shout "I'm a foster carer, he's not mine?". No, I took what I still feel was the best option. I put my arms out for him, I looked at him sympathetically and I scooped this little man into my arms.

As he sobbed and sobbed and showed me his finger, I could hear the tutting choirs again only this time as well as my own embarrassment I was also fearful. Yes, fearful of the other parents, they didn't look a very forgiving bunch, not to mention being out of tune and out of sync with their tuts, and I was literally terrified that the fat f***ing bitch was going to appear from the padding and be identified by Neil with his remaining good fingers. Please, please don't let him point her out, I just can't handle confrontation from an angry parent today. I busily distracted Neil by checking that his finger wasn't actually broken or damaged, by giving him some more squash and by allowing him to continue to bury his head and wipe his snot on my top.

There was absolutely no sign of Owen during this debacle and on returning to the table for sustenance he was most surprised to see Neil sitting on my knee in tears. Owen seemed intent on finding out who had done this to his brother and it struck me then that perhaps he considered the only person allowed to hurt his brother was him. Neil was fine and no damage was done to his finger but our two hours was almost up and so rather than put them back out into the padded thing I thought it best for us to leave while we still could and without me having to try to defend my lion cubs from the bigger animals in the jungle. For the last time that day, we hopped and skipped from a public area to the tunes of the choral tutters but I realised at this point that I would always and without fear, stick up for, protect and defend these boys, even if they were going to be the death of me.

The three of us survived our second night together, with more TV, games, bath and stories but nothing had actually changed. They were no calmer, no less likely to hit each other, squabble or want to be first or last for everything. If I'm honest, I felt I had just transported myself to another planet and a place where literally nothing mattered. Does it matter if they kill each other? Does it matter if they kill me? Does it matter which of us is killed first or last? I think I would have preferred to have been first but even this seemed unimportant at this point in time. Does it matter if we don't eat any healthy foods for forty eight hours? Does it matter if they fall and hurt themselves? Does it matter if I get arrested for not protecting the safety of a child in my care? Well, I suppose on that point, yes it does matter and I will refer back to the book of Mumbo Jumbo to see if they have any of the answers for how to avoid this situation – I suspect not!

I don't expect you to really know me yet, although I hope you're getting a picture, but you do need to know that all of this is factually true, these things really did happen and have not been embellished for your reading. I am normally a pretty confident, fun, capable person and I wasn't naïve going into foster care. I knew or had a fair idea of what to expect and I knew that I was good with kids; even if I do say so myself. I knew I had a lot of love to give and I also knew that I was good at getting children to do well, be happy and be confident. So you see, when Owen and Neil had arrived, by the time we got to the end of day two, I was having a bit of a crisis of confidence. I just couldn't believe that two children, no matter where they had come from or how they had been brought up, could be this way. I don't like trying to find one word that could describe them concisely but if I had to choose one it would be indescribable. By comparison, the other foster children I have had following on from them, who were all equally traumatised or damaged in their own separate ways, were simply nothing like Owen and Neil. Certainly I became a little more practised in dealing with children but trust me there just is no comparison; as already stated though, by the end of our first full day together, I felt a protectiveness towards them that I couldn't possibly have foreseen.

Chapter 7
Head First

Day three and I was praying for a miracle. I had managed to get some sleep and was awoken to the sound of very convincing automatic gun fire. They were busy being snipers and shooting down some passers-by in the street below from their bedroom window using their fingers as weapons. I have to admit that in my waking moments I didn't see the harm in this as long as no one was actually getting hurt. I didn't feel it was the right moment to be discussing the dangers of gun crime with them. I eventually called out to them to let them know I was awake and they both came hurtling through into my room still with their finger guns that could fire off a round of over one hundred bullets at any moment. Owen was especially good at this sound whereas Neil's sounded a little more like he was just blowing a big raspberry. I feigned death upon being shot at repeatedly and this little game must have gone on for quite a while before I was fully awake and ready for a brand new day.

I had decided that a trip to the playground would be the best way for me to try to tire them out a bit and then, so as to keep them contained in one place and without fear of harming others, I had thought we could perhaps find a couple of DVDs and watch these at home. Was I being lazy? Not intentionally, I just couldn't bear the idea of a repeat of the previous days antics and I needed to avoid small public spaces.

A playground however is a public place, but I was prepared to take my chances; I wish I hadn't. From getting up, having a leisurely breakfast, getting into the car and to the park, I had the usual constant bickers of who sits where, who is first and last to get their shoes on or their coats on and who can get to the car first or last; we eventually got in the car, with them in their designated seats, and off we went. We arrived at the park and they shot out of the car before I think it had even stopped moving. I made a note to myself to discuss the dangers of this with them later. I knew there should be a button on the car door to prevent escapees but I hadn't the time to find it right now and once the engine was off I found myself needing to run to try to find them. I called them back to me, with a quiet yell, and told them that they could run about as much as they liked but to be careful of other people and to ensure that they could see me, on this bench that I was sitting on, at all times. They understood and off they went. The playground was fairly busy and there were many families, parents and young children about so I kept a keen eye on Owen and Neil as best as I could. They were up and down and onto everything, tearing around like children do and appearing to have a lot of fun, while surely burning off some energy. This is good, I thought!

I sat watching them and watching the world go by until I saw them both disappearing up the fully enclosed cylindrical tube that was a slide. I was fine with this at first as sometimes that can be fun, can't it, to go up the slide as well as down it but they weren't reappearing either at the top or the bottom. I sat watching and waiting for them to reappear until I noticed the queue of expectant parents waiting for their little ones who had entered the slide feet first, from the top, to appear down the slide. At this point, and as they all gathered at the bottom, starting to poke their heads up the slide I reluctantly accepted that I needed to intervene. I walked quickly to the bottom of the slide and called up to Owen & Neil "Can you come out please and let the other kids past". There was at this point just a solo tutter while most of the other parents had some sort of a sympathy with me even if silently thinking I was a terrible parent with awful children.

There was no reply and several people now looked at me expectantly to do something more. What more was I to do? Try to go up there myself and drag them down? I called up to them again and said that they needed to come out and let the other children through but still there was no answer and not even an echoed giggle. I was conscious that there were still children at the top of this slide, blissfully unaware of a blockage and excitedly entering the slide. I was cross with the boys by now and facing the dilemma as to whether or not to confess, to the ever increasing choir of tutters waiting for their precious children to reappear, that the boys causing the blockage were my foster children and that I therefore couldn't be held responsible for their actions.

Then came a significant bang from the middle of the tube and, as if fired from a gun, out shot a little girl no more than three years old and head first. Her parents scooped her up and perhaps justifiably scowled at me. I called up again to Owen and Neil "If you don't get out of there right now then there will be no treats this afternoon, no TV and nothing nice at all for a very long time". Harsh I know but I had already found that no amount of bribery worked with these boys, they simply didn't know how to care. More rumblings in the tube and out shot another boy who was thankfully unscathed by the experience of being flipped around in the tube and sent out head first. One by one, these poor unsuspecting children, their lives ruined by the experience of going head first down a slide that they had entered feet first, appeared at the bottom to be scooped up by their adoring but angrily tutting parents.

I think word had got out not to enter the slide and actually this particular piece of playground equipment had no one around it at all by now; just me, helpless at the bottom and Owen and Neil in the tube and unseen. I sat on the end of the slide and called up to them to come down and a muffled call came back from Owen I think saying "How cross are you?". Very, was the answer but I sat and thought about it and decided that in order to get them out I needed to pretend to not be in the least bit cross. Against my better judgement, and every bone in my body telling me that they needed to be told or they would never learn, I called up to them "I'm not cross but the other parents were. They've all gone now and so it's safe for you to come out".

They appeared out of the slide jubilant that they had managed to get up there and to stay there, showing me intently how they had gripped with their hands, knees and feet as if it was a feat to have achieved this; which it probably was. They explained how the slide was more fun to go down if you went head first, you went faster apparently, and that they were only trying to show younger kids how to have more fun. What startled me is that they were suddenly animated and engaging in their conversation. They were proud of their achievements in the tube and while there was absolutely no thought or consideration for the disruption caused, who was I to tell them that they couldn't help other kids have more fun? I didn't know where to begin with this and so as with everything else that had occurred in the last forty eight hours I chose to temporarily ignore it. My little Mountain Goats had returned to me and were just being the Kids that they knew how to be.

Days three, four and five and months three, four and five followed. I don't have enough time to write every little detail and story but suffice to say we got through it. I suppose it all became a little bit easier day by day. Although that said, don't forget that in the midst of all of this, they had to contend with a whole host of dramas surrounding their family life that couldn't help but impact on our home life. I think all foster children go through many stages and many feelings naturally dependent on their circumstances and what the future may or may not hold for them. One minute they want to be with you, the next they hate you with a passion and the next they are attached and never want to leave you but realise that one day they must. As adults we can't even begin to imagine how this must affect a child and their inner-most and probably unknown feelings but I do write this with a confidence and a certainty that even the shortest period of time with safety, security and love has a huge and positive impact on them.

The words "you're being ridiculous" featured heavily for many, many months not just with Owen and Neil but with all the children I'll refer to. There were tears and tantrums, my legs were black and blue for a month or so from being kicked at while holding onto a wanton escapee at the back door. My fridge freezer was pushed over, which took some angry six year-old strength I can tell you, cereal bowls were hurled, squash stains on the ceiling; don't ask or at least we'll come to that later. The point is that we all went through some really difficult and heart breaking moments in those first few months but the mist eventually began to clear. I hadn't been committed to an asylum and they were suddenly both doing fairly well in school and becoming two happy and contented little boys. They both had birthdays to celebrate and school successes, and while their futures were uncertain they seemed to have gained a resilience to push them on and we were, albeit temporarily, a safe little pride.

The need for being first or last never left them and probably never will, but it became considerably less important to either of them. Everyday for years I would take them to school and every alternate day I would stand at the classroom door of one or other of them. They never changed their designated seats in the car, their seats at the kitchen table or their beds.

You're Being Ridiculous!

Chapter 8
Mating Turtles

I was at work, the one thing that actually was consistent and kept me sane for all these months, and my mobile phone rang. I could see it was the school, again, and I considered not answering as I knew they only ever called if there was some kind of trouble. I had spent so much time in the Head Teacher's office that we had become friends. I decided I probably should answer the phone and sure enough Owen had been fighting and would I come in. I mean really, what's a playground scuffle between boys; and I found myself, while getting in the car to head for the school, wondering if he had won the fight. Of course face to face with the child and the Head Teacher in the office I give a very different demeanour and luckily for me Owen never said "but you told me to whack them back if they hit me first". I expressed that both he and I knew that fighting was wrong, that he mustn't do it and that he should run to find a teacher even if he was being pinned up against a wall.

The Head Teacher, to be fair, was pretty reasonable and truth be known I think she may have secretly condoned the whacking back but I guess she just had to follow the school rule book. So she said to Owen "This behaviour can't continue, Owen, I want you to think of me sitting on your shoulder. Whenever you can see trouble coming your way or whenever you feel that something is about to happen, I want you to imagine me on your shoulder and whispering in your ear, walk away Owen, walk away". I could see the grim expression on his face and his need to walk away right now but he had become savvy enough to nod and smile in the right places and to say the right things to appease us whining whinging adults. We left on a harmonious note and Owen took Miss Trunchbull, obviously that's not her name and nor is there any resemblance whatsoever, back home on his shoulder.

Later that evening, the boys were both sitting calmly watching the TV, we had achieved this at least within a few months, and I went in to see they were okay and to tell them I was going for a shower. Yes, you see this is how good things were, I could leave them unattended in the knowledge that they wouldn't kill one another for the duration of my showers. Anyway, they barely acknowledged me, they were so engrossed in whatever they were watching, but Owen also had this pained look on his face and tears in his eyes as if he was about to cry. I asked him if he was okay, I think the adverts must have come on or I would never have had a response to this question, and he groaned "I'm OK but Claire, my shoulder is really hurting and I can't make it go away". I said to him "Oh, Owen, what do you think you have done?" He sat, and he sat and I thought the conversation was over before it had started until he said after some serious pondering "I think it's Miss Trunchbull, she's on my shoulder and she's pretty heavy to carry around!" Neil looked across at his brother and said "I can't see her, what are you talking about?" So, Owen explained to Neil how it was that Miss Trunchbull was on his shoulder but the concept was beyond Neil, seemingly well beyond them both really, so I gallantly took the Head Teacher off his shoulder on the proviso that I could return her in the morning before school. What the boys didn't know is that Miss

Trunchbull was expecting a baby; no wonder poor Owen's shoulder was hurting. This little fact was seemingly announced to all the children the next day in school and so that evening at tea time I had some very interesting but unexpected questions to answer.

"Miss Trunchbull is having a baby" Neil announced when he got home from school "and I know who the dad is" he claimed. He was actually looking serious but I simply had no idea where this conversation was going. "It must be Owen" he declared, "you know, from yesterday and her being on his back". I couldn't think what to say or how he had come to this conclusion, particularly as their knowledge of these matters was I thought probably more detailed than it should have been. I said "Neil, that's just not possible and not true"; fortunately Owen wasn't in the room and didn't have to be party to this conversation, but

You're Being Ridiculous!

I realised that little Neil's knowledge of babies was perhaps not what I had thought it was.

Before I had the chance to think of an explanation that would suit a six year old he said, while hopping animatedly from one foot to another convinced he knew this for certain and barely able to get his words out because there was so many of them to come, "It is true, I know it's true, remember, we watched it on the TV the other day. Remember when the Turtles were playing in the sand and then one Turtle climbed on the other Turtle's shoulder and there was this groaning sound like Owen was doing last night when Miss Trunchbull was on his shoulder, and then there were babies – I know this is true". Oh my God! How do I solve this one? The idea of Miss Trunchbull as a mating Turtle was more than I could take and I was unable to suppress my giggles which only resulted in making Neil very cross with me. I pulled myself together, controlled my laughter and simply said "Neil, it's definitely not Owen's baby, it can't possibly be because Miss Trunchbull is not a Turtle and human beings don't have babies like that". As soon as I said this I was regretting it as I was now expecting the question of how the baby did get there but he seemed to accept my final word and to rapidly lose interest. I thought I was helping their education by allowing them to watch nature programmes but I'm prepared to admit I may have been wrong.

That was the first of the slightly difficult conversations after school that day and the other arguably harder question was saved for tea time. Neil had seemingly forgotten the idea of Miss Trunchbull and Owen being mating Turtles but he had other things on his mind.

You're Being Ridiculous!

Chapter 9
Tea Time Topics

We were sitting, in our designated seats, having our tea, which by this point in time was healthy and involved amongst other things a variety of vegetables; they had been convinced that, along with a goodnight's sleep, these too would help them grow.

I had been enjoying my tea, and they were too, but then out of nowhere and like a bolt of lightening came Neil's question, "Claire, what's a Dildo?" Seriously, how would you answer this? After nearly choking on a mouthful of broccoli my first fleeting thought was, what on earth are they teaching them in school? I said "Neil, where did you hear that word?" to which he replied "At school today, Billy and I were fighting, he kicked me, I kicked him, he kicked me back, so I kicked him back even harder and he then punched me and called me a Dildo". "Oh", I said, instantly seeing my opportunity to get out of this, "You know you and Billy really shouldn't have been fighting, you know it's wrong to fight, if he kicks you then you go and tell a teacher, you don't kick him back". The mother Turtle will give us both trouble I was thinking, " What were you fighting about anyway?" I purposefully made this spiel to him as long and as convoluted as was possible so as to try to avoid the original question. Neil tells me that he and Billy had been fighting over a football and Owen pitches in that Billy is an idiot and that Neil should learn to walk away. I felt quite proud of Owen and that some of what he'd been told had sunk in so that he was able to impart words of wisdom to his brother even if he wasn't yet quite able to walk away from a fight himself. The problem unfortunately had not disappeared and the question was asked again "So what is a Dildo anyway?" Neil asked. Could they tell I was feeling awkward? Is that why they persisted with the question? No, I could tell by their faces that this was a genuine need to know.

I should explain that when Owen and Neil first came to live with me, their knowledge, Owen's in particular, on these matters was far more than it should have been aged seven. That said, they always referred to their privates as their middles. Writing this I'm not sure how I should refer to them but you know the area I'm speaking of and they called them their middles. I knew this because they would make comments like, he kicked me in the middles or he's flashing his middles, various statements that had been made over the months and led me to understand what and where their middles were. I should also point out that I had every now and then tried to alert them to their correct anatomical names and they did know these, hence the use of their almost correct language in the trampoline incident in Chapter 1. So, the middles it was, and with a captive audience, both of them had stopped eating, my aim was to try to keep it brief. This is how the conversation went:

"A Dildo is just another word for fake middles". I knew I could say this as I had also heard them refer to fake middles on previous occasions but would this be enough to end the conversation? No chance! Neil, piped up "Oh, like the one that Mum had" he said, to which Owen replied "yeh, I remember, it was green", "no it wasn't" Neil said, "it was purple". "No" Owen said "it was definitely green", "No" Neil said, "I know it was purple", "it was green", "it was purple", "it was green", "it was purple", "it was green", "it was purple"! "ENOUGH" I yelled, not very quietly, "Does it matter what colour it was? Perhaps she had two?". I was mortified that we were even discussing dildos at the dinner table, but they both conceded that she must have had two and we carried on with our now cold tea. I had dared to think to myself that that hadn't been too bad; on a scale of one to ten I think I gave myself a six for having successfully answered the question, but there was more to come; isn't there always?

After a few minutes, I could see and hear the cogs whirring in their heads, Owen said very earnestly, "So, Claire, what does a dildo do?". Oh my goodness, really this can't be happening, I'm so completely unprepared and I mentally score myself a big fat zero before I have even answered. Neil was beside himself with laughter, having just taken a sip of his drink, he literally showered the ceiling with orange squash and had some unidentifiable piece of his tea coming out of his nose, but was still able to sing "Owen it rhymes, Dildo do, Dildo do, Dildo Dildo Dildo do!" Owen wasn't laughing, he wanted an answer and I was trying hard to stifle my giggles at Neil's poetic licence to the Dildo Song that will now remain with me forever. Back to my poker face - I have a really good poker face now, and I so wanted this to be over, so I made it as short and as sweet as I possibly could. Given that I had no time to think of the best thing to say, and I just know that you're out there with your clever answers, I simply said to Owen, with Neil now listening intently "it's just something that some grown ups can use as a part of sex". I felt this covered all possible angles and surely left little room for further questioning. It seemed to have the desired affect until Neil chipped in "So will my penis come off and turn green or purple?" Owen scoffed in a knowing sort of way and said to his brother "You're being ridiculous; of course not Neil, your penis won't come off from your body, will it Claire?". "No" I replied, "no, your penis will not come off and it will not turn green or purple". I chuckled to myself, not about the mortifying conversation we had just had but about the fact that after months of living with me Owen had used in almost the right context my favourite words – you're being ridiculous!

You're Being Ridiculous!

Chapter 10
My Lion Cubs

Life with my two lion cubs carries on and we are living in some kind of harmonious bliss. Tempers still fray from time to time but my inner dictator hasn't been seen for many months; generally speaking we are all happy. There is a bond and a love between us all that has been well and truly formed which, while we all know this won't be forever, we are content to live in the moment until the powers that be tell us otherwise. We are all in a wonderful easy routine, there are things that we say, do, sing and play everyday, the predictability of which has helped them both to settle, feel secure and loved.

Every weekday morning for years, I would wake them up at seven thirty with my own rendition of 'Singing in the rain – Good Morning' – it was just our thing and these memories and feelings that they evoke are precious to me and I hope that maybe they still are to Owen and Neil too. Ross the dog was very much a part of this little bubble that we inhabited and he was walked by us all daily and was right there with us when things were calm but would still retreat to his bed if voices were ever raised.

A lot of fun was had out on dog walks, in the woods or out in the countryside. There were huge arsenals of stick weaponry littered around and there was a lot of tree climbing from Owen, but with Neil choosing to keep both feet on the ground. He did once attempt to follow Owen up a tree and he followed him up okay but then got stuck and couldn't go up or down. He really did freeze and there was nothing I could do. I encouragingly tried to tell him how to sit, kneel or perch and where he could place his feet but he got himself into such a state and was so upset that he started to scream at me "I can't get down and you just want me dead". "You're being ridiculous" I called up to him. "If you won't listen to my advice then you're just going to have to stay up in the tree". I asked Owen to come down and to help him in the hope that Neil would take advice from his brother otherwise I honestly didn't see how I was going to get him down. I really couldn't watch, he was so high up and I reluctantly turned my back rather than actually see the potential fall. I listened from afar, with tears in my eyes, to the calm and actually genuinely loving way in which they spoke to each other. Neil did make it down and

Owen was pleased to have helped him. They may still fight like lion cubs but do you know, watching the bond between these brothers grow was one of the most precious and rewarding things to witness and to have been a part of.

There are so many more tales to tell, so many more one liners that they came out with that made us all laugh and cry but I can't possibly relay them all and there are other children for me to introduce you to. What I can say to you is that by the time Owen and Neil left my care, they were quite simply delightful boys. Of course I'm biased, they were still slightly roguish, I suspect they always will be, but they had big hearts, they were clever when they chose to be, they were all the things that you would want your own children to be. I don't mind admitting that I truly loved them and I always will. I no longer see them but not a day goes by when I don't think of them and I hope that one day, when they are all grown up, they may come back into my life with some favourite memories of their own.

You're Being Ridiculous!

Chapter 11
The IT Expert

I needed a bit of adjustment time to get over what was a much bigger loss than I had anticipated I could ever feel. The lion cubs were safely away but the house was so empty and quiet and I had no one wittering in my ear from morning to night. My poor old Ross also had to be put down around this time but what a hero he had been for me over the years. It was old age that got him eventually and I spent a few months getting used to life without Owen, Neil and Ross. I took the most wonderful holiday, partly to drown my sorrows but also to live a little again; I'm no saint I can assure you! When I returned from holiday to my empty, silent home, I decided it was time to get another dog. I felt the need for a reliable man in my life, one that sleeps downstairs and doesn't paw at me at night, one that only requires feeding out of a tin twice a day and gives me unconditional love. Welcome, Bailey! Another rescue dog, slightly less neurotic than Ross, but just as lovable. Bailey became a big part of my home and life within days.

A few months went by and over the next year or so I had several short term foster placements. These varied from just a few days to a few weeks. The children are simply children, but still children with varying problems. They all need to feel safe, secure and loved and even after my rookie experiences with Owen and Neil I felt I was ready to go again.

You're Being Ridiculous!

First up, would you believe it, were two more brothers Josh and William. Josh was nine and William was eight. This placement was a little more planned than the first and I had been given information on the brothers so felt ready when they arrived. I had been shopping, I wasn't falling into that trap again. They were coming to me mid-week and they had been in care before so they were old hands at this; arguably more so than me.

At this point though, and having only experienced Owen and Neil, I was on high alert in anticipation of their imminent arrival. The doorbell rang, I opened the door and I was met by two bubbly smiling boys, eager to come in but waiting to be asked. They breezed in followed by their social worker and they went straight into the sitting room to see a very excitable Bailey who greeted them with wagging tail and copious licks. After a few minutes, the boys seemed fine, I was fine and the social worker left. What a huge difference this was. Everyone was calm, but scarred by my initial previous experience I was still ready and waiting for this to change.

We went through to the kitchen and I got them both a drink and a snack. As we sat at the kitchen table, in undesignated seats, Josh said to me "Do you know you're Wi-Fi isn't working?" I didn't know my Wi-Fi wasn't working, I thought it was, or at least it had been the last time I checked, anyway how on earth can he possibly know? So I said, "I didn't realise it wasn't working, Josh, how do you know this?" to which he replied "When we came in I could see there were only two lights on the hub and not three, there should be three". "Really", I said, "show me". Bailey was under our feet and so I opened the back door for him, put him out into the garden and closed the door. I wanted to be able to give these boys my time and without constant interruption from an overexcited dog. So, the three of us traipsed back into the sitting room, to check out the Wi-Fi.

I need to make it clear that while I consider myself to be computer literate, I would probably say so in a job application, I am not by any means a technical whizz; in fact technology terrifies me and sometimes really irks me. I don't do all this social media stuff, probably because I'm verging on the anti-social and I really just use my laptop for work, e-mails, storing photos, the internet, writing a book – all very basic stuff. If anything ever goes wrong, I switch off and switch on again and this usually does the trick. If it's a bigger IT problem than that then I'm able to Google it and I can often find the answer this way. Anything to do with the lovely BT or Wi-Fi though and I feel the fear setting in that I'm going to have to spend hours that I don't have on the phone to a call centre and while I'm incredibly tolerant with most things, this can tip me over the edge.

Josh pointed out the two lights and the light that was off. He told me it should be glowing either green or blue. William chipped in that it should be blue and not green and Josh, starting to get slightly irate with his younger brother, told me that it depends on the make and the model of the hub and that it might be that the light is blue or green. I smiled to myself, remembering Owen and Neil with their squabble about dildo colours but quickly got back to the task in hand with these earnest polite little boys trying to help with a problem that I didn't even know I had. Josh suggested that I check my connectivity, I presumed he meant with the internet and so I went to get my laptop. It was on my mind that I really should start to prepare their tea for them but even I was curious now to see if Josh was right and to see if I had a problem. I started the laptop up, it's fairly old and takes a while to get going, a bit like me on occasions, but Josh then started to tell me that my hard drive may need replacing and how many RAMs was it and what was the storage capacity? He's nine for heaven's sake, and actually his knowledge, while impressive and far superior to mine, was beginning to annoy me. I know that sounds terrible but I didn't know the answers to his questions. If he asked me about mating Turtles or parts of the anatomy, fake or otherwise, then we possibly could have conversed. I didn't know about RAMs or Gigabytes and quite frankly all I really wanted to do was establish if I had a problem and then go and cook their tea.

I did have a problem and I wasn't connected. "I can fix that for you" Josh said. "Oh, thanks Josh but don't worry" I replied, really not wanting to give this child free use of my laptop. Could he really do this? Is he not too young to know how to figure something like this out? I actually didn't know. William stuck up for his brother and said "You know, he really does know how to do stuff like this, he does it at home for our Mum all the time". I needed to start cooking the tea, so I asked them to just wait a couple of minutes and said that when I'm ready we can sit down together and look at it. I wanted to see what he could do.

The tea was cooking and we resumed our places side by side on the sofa. Josh had the laptop, I had entered the password, checking that he wasn't watching me type. I had a feeling that if he was wise enough to fix the problem then he'd be clever enough to fleece me too. My usual willingness to see the good in everyone had been put on hold while I watched this young man do his thing. He was on the internet tapping away on what looked like a discussion forum, then to the BT website, he downloaded a Helpdesk thing and he methodically went through the stages that they recommended. He occasionally asked me to tell him what a word said and then, well blow me down, he'd fixed it. After only a few clicks and a detailed explanation from Josh, accompanied by the explanation in layman terms from William, who seemed equally computer savvy, I still didn't really comprehend any of what they were telling me. It was something to do with band width and KHz but the light went blue so apparently I should have known that I had the oldest model of hub and that it might be a good idea for me to upgrade. The cooker alarm went off and I was back on schedule with the tea but was left in utter amazement at the abilities of these boys.

You're Being Ridiculous!

Chapter 12
Washing and Walking

We had our tea, they whinged a little about steak pie and vegetables and mentioned subtly for tomorrow night that their favourite and usual tea was Doughnuts. I tried to suggest that this perhaps wasn't a very nutritious diet but they were both glazing over and rolling their eyes at me so I moved the conversation on to more exciting things. With tea finished, we played a board game and there were, to my delight, no squabbles, punching or shrieking. They both then wanted showers as opposed to a bath and were thankfully slightly more body conscious and shy than my previous boys. They knew how to use a towel too but as with the vast majority of the male population, in my experience anyway, they thought it's rightful place following their shower was the bathroom floor along with their dirty washing. I can forgive them this as truthfully they were a joy to have around, and to have had my internet fixed so expertly was a huge bonus. I'm not sure how I would have fixed the problem if left to my own devices; it quite possibly would have taken me days.

Bed time was easy, there was no first and last up the stairs and there were no squabbles about which beds to be in, they made their choices for stories and we sat and read these. As we were reading I could smell this smell that was unfamiliar and I made a mental note to myself to investigate when I had finished their stories. I carried on reading to them but the smell was becoming over-powering and was really beginning to bother me. Both boys were showered and clean, so it wasn't them. The dog isn't allowed upstairs but had he somehow got in to their room? Oh no! The dog, he's still outside, he hasn't had his tea, he's been shut outside for over three hours, how could I have forgotten him? I began to hurry through the book, feeling guilty that Bailey would be feeling abandoned and feeling guilty that I was hurrying their story when they had been so good. No longer a rookie carer but still guilt ridden that I seemingly can't manage to even look after my dog and what is that smell?

With the books finished, the three of us had a little more of a chat and I thanked them both again for fixing my Wi-Fi. I had already decided that Bailey could just wait a few more minutes and I didn't want to hurry the lights out and my exit from the room as they were being so good. I still could not believe how easy they were and how uncomplicated they seemed. They told me what time their school started in the morning and William mentioned that he needed his PE kit from the bag in the corner of the room. That's it! That is where the smell was coming from, I hadn't really noticed that they had a bag when they arrived. It was a big bag, stuffed full of clothes, it looked as if they were staying for a month and not the planned few days.

When I unzipped it, I was hit by this stench that I'm not even going to try to describe. I suggested that I take the bag downstairs and sort through it but both boys seemed reluctant for me to take away their possessions. They climbed out of their beds and started to pull everything out of the bag; there was absolutely nothing in there apart from dirty smelly clothes. I asked them if I could take it all to wash it but no, this wasn't acceptable. Why? I'll never know. Perhaps they thought I wouldn't give it back or that I'd shrink things? We agreed on the items of clothing that they would need for the next day, school clothes, PE kits and I was allowed to take these to wash ready for the morning. It was also solemnly agreed that if I returned these to them in the morning they would then let me take a few more items to wash. It's hard to explain and it's even harder to truly understand but they were both adamant I was not to be trusted with all their washing in one go and without their supervision.

I was armed with a pile of dirty stinking laundry; they were now back in their beds and I gave them both a kiss goodnight. Josh wanted a hug, William didn't but he seemed to be quite happy. I turned out the light, pulled the door to and went downstairs. I hurried to the back door to find my poor Bailey. He was sitting there waiting patiently but quite blatantly had the hump with me as he went straight to his bed and turned his back on me. What had I said about unconditional love from a dog – it appears not! I put the allotted load of washing on and went back to Bailey to try to make my amends. It took him all of two seconds to forgive me and he ate his tea, three hours late, while I went to check if my hub light was still blue!

Josh and William were good sleepers and they had to be woken the following morning at seven thirty. Quite how they slept with the stench of the remaining unwashed clothes I'll never know. William sprang out of bed, demanding to see his clean clothes. Josh was less springy and needed a bit of cajoling and bribery to get him out. I'm delighted to report that they were both satisfied with my ability to wash and iron and they willingly handed over the remainder for me to do. I threw open their bedroom window feeling the need for fresh air and then scooped up the remaining dirty clothing. The boys were successfully delivered to school, no need for designated seats in the car and they were happy just to be dropped at the school gates in their clean clothes and William with his clean PE kit.

There are things we know about the children who come to us in care and there are many things we don't know. I certainly hadn't been made aware that Josh was some kind of a computer genius. It's possible of course that he's not and that every nine year old could have done what he did but it seemed pretty clever to me and I was very sorry I had ever doubted him. Why was William so protective of his clothing? I'll never know and I can't work it out.

William adored Bailey and was desperate to walk him as frequently as we could in the few days that they were with me. We all went for a walk one day along the river and this is where William showed his true colours. He's definitely the comedian. A lady came past us jogging with ear phones in and William decided he would jog in her shadow. It was very spontaneous and very funny. You had to be there I guess and my writing won't do it justice but he was quick enough that every time she perhaps sensed or felt there was someone behind her he would run to the opposite side of where she was looking. So if she glanced over her right shoulder he would duck to the left and vice versa. He kept this up with a type of comedy quickstep run for at least a hundred yards. She eventually caught him out, stopped and took out her ear phones; he was way ahead of Josh and I so I don't know what was said but she smiled and waved cheerily to us; she wasn't a tutter!

These boys were adorable, wise beyond their years and very brave. They were only with me for a few days but we had great fun and they absolutely renewed my belief in fostering and in what I was trying to do with my time and love. While I have no idea what has become of Josh and William I can only hope that they go on to lead successful lives, without too much baggage from their pasts. I wonder if one day I may see them as the next Bill Gates or a modern day budding actor or comedian.

You're Being Ridiculous!

Chapter 13

Hummus or Couscous?

Brian, Brian, Brian! I just don't know what I can tell you about Brian. He was a complicated little soul who was just with me for a weekend but what a long weekend it was. Not as long and no where near as traumatic as my rookie experience but nevertheless it was difficult. Brian wouldn't speak much and he wouldn't eat anything that I had in the house and I mean nothing. I was well prepared at all times by this point and I had every conceivable food type, or so I thought, that any child could possibly want, good or bad for them.

Brian arrived on a Friday evening, I was beginning to think that some parents and social workers conspired to do this so they could all enjoy their weekends and get the kids' washing done. Brian seemed fairly sullen but not actually upset. I tried to chat with him but was getting nothing back. I asked him what he might like for his tea but there was no response so I was coming up with ideas and alternatives that he might accept but he shook his head to everything. I had exhausted the options contained in my fridge, freezer and kitchen cupboards. So, I made us some beans on toast, I mean who doesn't like beans on toast? He'd been given other choices from cordon bleu to crisps and so in my exasperation, beans on toast felt like the easiest option to me and was quite frankly all I could be bothered to cook for myself by now. As I sat eating my tea, with

Brian having pushed away his plate without even looking at it or me, I began to worry again. How was I to keep him alive for forty eight hours if he wasn't going to eat? I remembered I had once read somewhere that as long as you drink water you can survive for several days so I concluded that if he wasn't going to tell me what he wanted to eat then he would at least survive his time with me by drinking fluids.

I finished my beans on toast giving an exaggerated "yum, yum, that was delicious", just to prove a point although again, I'm not sure what point this was that I was trying to prove. As I sat eating a yoghurt, which he had also refused, I was babbling away at him to try to find something that would spark a smile, a laugh or even a hint of interest at anything I was saying. I also began wondering if he was feeling, as I had felt with Owen & Neil, that he wished I could just be quiet for five minutes so that he could formulate his plan of how to keep me quiet permanently. My yoghurt finished, I was just thinking to myself what on earth are we to do now, when Brian stood up from the kitchen table, went to the cupboard and took out a little mini box of raisins. I made no comment. I had by this point decided that my babbling away was not going to make him speak and I let him sit and pick at his raisins in peace. The first time he spoke was to ask for more raisins and of course I happily agreed thinking that even if he just ate raisins we would definitely make it through the weekend and there was no way he could possibly starve. Bailey was fed, had done everything he needed to do in the garden and was safely back on his bed, undisturbed by Brian.

Compared to my previous first nights, the minutes and hours this evening could not have gone by any slower. Still in the kitchen and with two empty boxes of raisins on the table I said to him "Brian, would you like to have anything more to eat?" He shook his head. "Well, when I have finished clearing up, would you like to play a game? We could play a board game, you can go in the sitting room and pick one if you like?" He stared at me and shook his head. "Would you like to watch TV?" Again, he just shook his head. Now, he wasn't visibly upset, but of course he was obviously troubled by being in my home and not wherever he thought he should be, so trying to ensure that he was happy in some sort of way was like pulling teeth. "There are some books upstairs, would you like to go and pick one and I could read it to you or if you don't want me to read to you then you can look at it yourself?" He stared, he stared for longer than was comfortable and shook his head. "I know" I said, still trying to be cheery, "would you like to have a bath or a shower and get into your pyjamas?" He stared, he stared and he stared some more. I was actually beginning to feel as if the devil himself was in my house and that I was about to be bludgeoned – I joke but actually this has happened to some carers. Brian then spoke in a Jack Nicholson, "here's Johnny" kind of way and said "Do you think I'm a baby or something? I'm ten and you shouldn't speak to me unless you're spoken to". Wow, he speaks, it's scary and I was fairly sure he had his own age wrong and this confused me somewhat. I was sure I had been told he was seven, he only looked seven, could we all have got this wrong? Unable, while at least engaged in some sort of a conversation, to get to the sideboard to look at the paperwork I had been given on his arrival, I made the assumption that this was some sort of a test and also by now I was rather indignant at being told I shouldn't speak unless I was spoken to.

Feeling brave and feeling as if I shouldn't have to justify myself to a seven or ten year old,

I said "Brian, there's no need to speak to me like that, I can speak in my own home". "Fair enough", he said "but I don't have to listen, you're not the boss of me". Bring back the silence I thought, this is all I need. "Anyway" I said, "I don't think you're ten are you, I thought you were seven?". "You're just being obtuse" he said. Really, I don't believe it, how does a seven or ten year old even know that word; and I'm not being obtuse, am I? I could feel myself getting cross and tried to disguise it by walking away to the sideboard, flicking through the papers I had been given to search for the information I needed. There it was in black and white, date of birth. I did my best at my mental maths, hiding the use of my fingers from him, wishing I had tried harder in school, and yes, sure enough he was seven. To be precise seven and two months. I nonchalantly turned around and busied myself with something else before saying "I think you are seven Brian, and you should enjoy being seven, it's a great age to be". "When will you learn?" he said to me holding his head in his hands and I wondered what was coming next. How was this little boy going to chastise me further? Much to my annoyance, I decided to obey him. I would no longer be obtuse and I had learnt my lesson. I got the newspaper that I hadn't yet had time to read and we sat in silence across the kitchen table. I don't think I read a word as I could feel his eyes boring into my head and I was desperately trying to think of a way out of this silence but to no avail. We sat, I muttered every now and then, trying not to annoy him any more than I already had, until it really was a reasonable time for him to get to bed.

I showed him his bedroom and where the bathroom was. I asked if he wanted any help to get into his pyjamas or brushing his teeth. He declined by shaking his head, and this was fine by me as I indignantly felt that at seven or ten, he should be old enough to manage. I asked if he wanted me to read him a story when he was ready and I got the stare, so at risk of being told off again I went and sat on my bed waiting for him to get changed, brush his teeth and get into his bed. Safely tucked in and having refused a story, he suddenly said to me "I will eat Hummus, Couscous, Sesame seeds, things like that so perhaps we could have that tomorrow?" Now who's being obtuse, I thought to myself but what I actually said was "Well, after breakfast then perhaps we can go to the shop and buy a couple of things that you would like. I do want you to be happy Brian". He looked at me, with a slightly softer stare and said "Good night Claire, I hope you get some rest!". Rest! Do I look like I need a rest? I braced myself for attack but asked if he wanted a goodnight kiss and to my surprise he agreed so with a quick kiss on the cheek I said "Good night Brian, I'll see you in the morning!"

I turned out the light and chuckled down the stairs. Get some rest indeed!

Do I need rest? What on earth was happening? Have I been transported back in time to the days where children were seen and not heard or when wives obeyed their husbands. I joke, but truthfully I suspect I wasn't far off the mark as this little boy had a way with words that I have never heard before and I can only imagine where it had come from.

Chapter 14
A Glorious Morning

The morning came and Brian sauntered in. "Wake up sleepyhead" he said "it's the most glorious morning and we should do something fun". Fun, I thought, fun, where am I? Am I dreaming that I'm a part of the Famous Five? Fun does not happen at, I check the clock, six thirty in the morning. Well, at least he is being civil and has obviously pardoned me for my obtuseness. I made a decision that I would never usually make at this hour. Yes, I suppose I was allowing this seven year old child who thought he was fifty never mind ten to bully me into getting up at this ridiculous hour on this apparently glorious morning but I have to admit I was slightly intrigued as to what possible fun we could have.

I strolled downstairs still in my pyjamas; it was not a glorious day, it wasn't even light yet. Slightly angry at myself for having been duped by a seven year old, I started to make a cup of tea. As the kettle was boiling, I realised Brian hadn't followed me down stairs, so from the bottom of the stairs I called up "are you coming down Brian?". "I'm just getting dressed" he replied. Oh no! I had visions of him appearing for breakfast in his best suit and tie and expecting some kind of a Downton Abbey type breakfast with sardines or a poached egg? Actually, I think I had offered him this last night amongst other things but there was no way on earth I was offering it again. Down he came, thankfully he wasn't dressed smartly but

You're Being Ridiculous!

I still felt like a slob padding around in my pyjamas and bare feet. I couldn't help myself and I said "Brian, what made you think it was such a glorious day?". Silence! Was I being obtuse again? Good, I had meant to be! Claire, come on, pull yourself together I thought to myself, he's just a seven year old boy.

We sat, me with my bowl of Branflakes and Brian with an empty bowl and an empty plate while I waited for him to come to his own decision as to whether or not he wanted cereal or toast or both. Neither was the answer and so by this point, on my second cup of tea - and it was still just past seven o'clock - I had a fear of the day ahead and that it was going to be a long one. I asked again if he would like to watch TV or play a game and felt marginally as if progress was being made when I at least got an answer, even if that answer was no. This morning Brian seemed to be taking more of an interest in Bailey, but I have to confess this concerned me a little as I felt that poor Bailey might be being lulled into a false sense of security and was going to be used in a plot or ritual as some sacrificial animal to teach me a lesson in how not to be obtuse. When I was ready to go and get dressed, I put Bailey out into the garden, shut the door, locked it and took the key with me. This is being written tongue in cheek, although very truthfully; I know you may think I'm being harsh, and amidst it all I have every compassion for any child in my care but equally as a carer it's up to me to keep them safe and I honestly just couldn't be sure that Brian wouldn't do something silly in the few minutes it would take me to get dressed and ready for our fun day.

I'll skip the trip to a supermarket, it was thankfully non-eventful and he seemed pleased with his various choices of healthy foods that I didn't even know existed.

Fortunately most of it looked like it came out of a packet or tub and so I didn't think much culinary skill was going to be required. I'm not sure what the Sesame seeds were for; in fact I think I still have them at the back of a cupboard.

So, our fun on this glorious day consisted of walking the dog and a trip to an old aeroplane museum. He told me that parks were for babies, soft play centres had too many silly children in them and swimming was not a life skill that he had learned yet – his words not mine.

Still not even ten o'clock in the morning, and not a particularly glorious day; we set off in the car with Bailey in the boot highly excited that we appeared to be doing something that involved him. I had decided that as my Saturdays wouldn't usually even begin until around this time this needed to be a very long walk to while away a significant part of the day.

You're Being Ridiculous!

A long walk we had, Bailey was ecstatic, and Brian and I trudged through the woods and along a river bank, not quite in silence but almost. He seemed just not to know how to have fun. In trying to make it exciting for him, by running, jumping or swinging from a tree, I'm too old for this really, all I did was make him think I was more of a fool than he had already concluded. I gave up in the end and we walked side by side like an old married couple except he wouldn't even hold my hand.

We were home by lunchtime and sat, Bailey exhausted on his bed, and had some Couscous or something unidentifiable to me but to my delight enjoyable for Brian. I swear he almost smiled and said "yum, yum!".

The afternoon was spent at the aeroplane museum. According to Brian, this was somewhere that he had always wanted to go but so rarely had the time – again, his words, not mine. It was free to enter but donations were requested so I popped some money in the box and in we went. An elderly gentleman, who was presumably a volunteer and I suspect a war veteran, approached us and pointed out all of the things to see and do. Brian listened intently to him; he didn't find him obtuse, in fact he chatted animatedly about the history of World War I or II as I stood beside them both, trying to keep up with this rather intellectually stimulating conversation whilst really wishing I was still at home in my pyjamas. To be fair, I was pleased that he was able to converse so eloquently and respectfully to this man but then to my horror and guilt I was mortified when the gentleman pulled me aside and said "what a well mannered, clever boy your son is. You should be very proud". I was waiting for Brian to say, she's not my Mum or words to that affect but he didn't, he looked proud and so as not to appear obtuse to either of these gentlemen, I thanked him for his kind words and we moved swiftly on.

The museum was not my idea of fun on a glorious day but it was the first time I had seen Brian move with any childlike speed and so I suffered it. He was up into the planes, telling me what all the controls did, although I don't think he really had a clue, but maybe he did. Who knows what or how much kids know about something? I wasn't prepared to question him, not just for fear of being chastised but more so because he was actually having fun....on this glorious day!

We had been there for over two hours and it wasn't a big museum. My legs were starting to ache from the marathon walk in the morning and from running up and down steps into various cockpits. I had tried to suggest several times in the last half an hour, without sounding obtuse, that we should maybe think about setting off home for tea. Although realistically setting off home for Couscous or Hummus or whatever it was we had for tea didn't seem that appealing either. Anyway, my subtlety had been ignored and so I started to be slightly more insistent. The elderly gentlemen, the volunteer, not Brian, had very nicely come over to me at about three thirty and told me that they usually shut at four o'clock; it was now five to four and Brian was defiantly still not ready to leave.

I had followed him up into the cockpit of some old World War II plane that was so tiny I couldn't stand up straight in it. I sat next to Brian, him as the pilot and me as the co pilot. He was looking pretty cross by now as he knew why I was there. He said to me very clearly "I am not ready to leave yet and you are not the boss of me, you should think very carefully before you speak." I'm thinking.....I'm still thinking.... What do I say? I wanted to haul him out of there by the scruff of his neck but I can't, I'm a foster carer, we are nice and calm and la de dah! So here's what happened. I said to him "Brian, we have to go home as the nice man you were talking to earlier wants us to leave because they are closing up for the night. I have had such a fun day, Brian, so let's not ruin it by having a disagreement now". The la de dah is going well so far. "I know" I said, "why don't we pretend we are in the war and that you land this plane through enemy fire. Then when we have landed, so as not to get captured, we have to run as fast as we can, while being shot at the whole time. We can pretend that my car is an army tank and that we reach this safely and evade our enemy." He was silent again, he stared at me with that unnerving stare for what seemed like an eternity, until he suddenly shouted, "May day, May day, we have been shot, engine failure". I started to panic until I remembered we were on the ground. Good, this was good, he was going with this idea. "Enemy territory, prepare for crash landing." I think I did actually brace myself and when he said "Bang" I jumped. He vaulted out of the cockpit, I stumbled out, my knees and legs not working properly due to the tiny space I had been squeezed into. The elderly man was coming towards us, presumably with his final request for us to leave and he looked alarmed to see me chasing Brian across the field as he ran, ducking and dodging bullets. I waved to the man and called goodbye as I puffed after Brian. I too was running, ducking and dodging bullets, in fact I think I was maybe shot in the leg as I had a terrible pain. We arrived, me out of breath, back at the army tank and stupidly thinking the game was over I dared to draw breath and laugh at my own stupidity but Brian had other ideas and our escape was not over yet. He jumped into the back seat of the car and said "drive man, drive." I got in, legs like jelly from over exertion or from being shot, I still wasn't sure, started the engine and drove away. "Slow down boy, slow down" Brian yells at me from the back, "army tanks can only go about 25 miles per hour and you're already doing 30." How had I gone from man to boy in 0 to 30? I wasn't sure I wanted to play any more but we drove at 25 miles per hour until I could bear it no longer and I put my foot down. "That was a really fun game Brian" I said, to which he replied "it wasn't a game, I'm too old for games".

I do wonder what has happened to Brian? I can't even begin to imagine and there's a bit of me that wishes he had been with me for a little longer so I could really show him how to have fun on a glorious day.

Chapter 15
Excuse Me

More brothers! Who do all the little girls go to and why do I get all the boys? Max and Tom, five and three, arrive and they are as cute as can be. They are lively as you would expect but they don't appear to be phased by their new surroundings or by me. Actually, their entire stay is very easy and so I find myself with little to write about. This may well be a short chapter.

We had a lot of fun on glorious days in the few weeks they were with me and they certainly didn't seem to find me obtuse. I took them on various trips here, there and everywhere. They loved the beach, they loved swimming, they loved the park, it's fair to say that these two boys loved life and surely that's the way it should be for any child.

Max thought he was a pirate and that we should all be shipmates and this was always fine until it came to bedtime and I tried to remove his eye patch and imaginary parrot. He was a sweet boy, slightly shy but he kept me amused and my kitchen floor had never been so clean with the amount of times I was asked to scrub the decks. Tom was just Tom! He was three and did what all three year olds do. He was great fun, he also was made to scrub the decks which he did perhaps more often and more obligingly than me. The most endearing but equally annoying thing I remember about Tom was that he had been taught to say "excuse me" when he wanted to ask something and this came out as "coomee!" It was funny and endearing the first few times but believe me, on a car journey of more than five minutes or when I was trying to get on with something at home, it became not so cute and almost unbearable. He would say "Coomee" before he said anything at all and given that he had an awful lot that he wanted to say I was "coomeed" out by the time they left.

I would love to think that Max and Tom, particularly given their young age, are settled somewhere now and forever. They were two truly gorgeous boys.

You're Being Ridiculous!

Chapter 16
Kevin-says-no

Along came Kevin! This was at very short notice but by now I was always prepared. Ready for that sudden phone call from social work and ready with food in the house, toothbrushes, spare clothes and anything that may be required for a last minute placement. That is unless I was asked to take in a girl and then I would be well and truly in trouble, not least because I had no girls' clothes but also because I'm not sure now that I would be able to think of what to play, and God forbid if I had to plait hair. What if it were two sisters and they both required ambidextrous hair washes? Well, I'll cross that bridge when it arises.

So back to Kevin. He was seven and he arrived, not happy at all, in fact screaming and resisting entry into the house. His social worker had a good healthy firm grip of him and gave him a gentle nudge over the threshold. Already this was new to me as I hadn't had a child that didn't willingly come in. Some came in too willingly but this was the complete opposite. Kevin absolutely one hundred per cent did not want to be here. I think at this stage it was easy enough for me not to take it personally as he didn't know me yet or my apparent obtuseness. I had to assume it wasn't me that he'd taken a dislike to, but this new situation he had found himself in. The social worker came in, again it was a Friday evening, and though very pleasant she was obviously in a hurry to get away for her weekend. Lucky her

I say, and I hope for my sake that she made the most of it.

Kevin was no longer upset, just angry. Very, very angry. He met Bailey and was quite taken with him. There's definitely something very therapeutic for all of us, but especially children, when things are bothering them, in stroking a dog and being given their undivided attention but with no words. I offered Kevin a drink and he chose to have a hot chocolate, so I made this for him wondering what my next move was going to be. I didn't try to engage him in mindless chit chat, I just left him for a few minutes to try to calm down and stroking the dog seemed to be having the desired affect. He was by now actually lying right beside the dog in his bed and with his head buried in the dog's neck but I thought it best to let this happen as Bailey didn't seem to mind too much and Kevin was seemingly coming to terms with his current situation.

With the hot chocolate made, I told Kevin it was ready for him on the table whenever he wanted it. He got up, covered in dog hair, and sat at the kitchen table. I noticed for the first time that he was really a very sweet looking boy. I mean all kids look sweet don't they, but actually he was quite handsome. I gave him a few options for what he might like for his tea and to my delight he opted for beans on toast. I know you think you are seeing a theme here, or my inability to cook a proper meal, but I promise you I can cook, it's just that these first nights and days need to be more about comfort and settling-in food as opposed to healthy living.

Now up to this point Kevin had really said very little. In fact I think all he had said was that he would like beans on toast. As we sat eating, I posed the question, "What would you like for a pudding?" A simple question I thought and a nice one too but the answer I got was a very cross "Kevin-says-no". "Coomee!", I thought to myself. How does that even make sense, Kevin says no? So I said "So, you don't want a pudding then? You could have a yoghurt or some fruit?". "Kevin-says-no" came the reply again, followed immediately by "yes, yoghurt please". Now I was really confused. I seemed to have a child that was saying a firm no to everything but then saying yes immediately after. I gave him his yoghurt and he devoured it in seconds. Clearly we have some communication issues! Kevin says no to everything, and I mean literally everything. If it's something he does want then it will be followed by a yes but if it's something he really doesn't want or wish to do then there's no yes, just "Kevin-says-no". I can't begin to write it all down but Kevin said no and then sometimes yes, to playing a game, watching TV, having a bath, brushing his teeth, getting ready for bed, having a story, the list goes on and every single answer to the question or the request was "Kevin-says-no". I started to feel as if I was looking after Jim Trot, the character in The Vicar of Dibley who says no, no, no, no, no – yes! My reply when I realised this wasn't a one off, you may or may not be surprised to learn was not, "you're being ridiculous", but was simply "Claire-says-yes". For days our conversations went like this and it wasn't easy. So, if I was to say "Kevin, could you go and get ready for bed?" the reply would be "Kevin-says-no" and my reply would be "Well, Claire-says-yes". It seemed like it was an automatic response for him and I think it only finally began to subside when he realised that nine times out of ten I was asking him to do something nice or fun, to which the answer naturally ended up being yes, and so he dropped the "Kevin-says-no" and I was eventually able to drop the "Claire-says-yes".

You're Being Ridiculous!

Kevin-says-no, I will always think of him as this, was actually a very sweet boy. It's fair to say that he did not want to be in foster care but he coped well with it for the few weeks he was with me. He became considerably less angry and we had some good times. Kevin was in school, and as with many children in care, they actually love being at school and see it as a bit of a safe haven; he was a clever, slightly cheeky boy and this was proven in the last few days of his time with me. I was working and so our morning routine was that we would both have breakfast together, I would take him to school, see him into the playground at about eight fifty in the morning and then drive to work for 9 o'clock. It had all been working brilliantly or so I thought, until I got a call from the school secretary asking me who to invoice for Kevin's Breakfast Club. Slightly confused, I explained that Kevin hadn't been at the Breakfast Club since he had been with me and that there must be some mistake. She sounded bemused herself as to how or why the error had occurred but she accepted what I was saying and we rang off. Ten minutes later the head teacher called me back and after a brief discussion, with me adamant that Kevin had been having his breakfast at home and her adamant that he had been having breakfast at school, with the intervention of the lady that runs the Breakfast Club she was able to confirm that Kevin had been telling her daily that his foster carer didn't give him breakfast. I was mortified! Neither I nor they, after my protestations, could believe that he had the cheek to do this and the idea of Kevin-says-no getting a double breakfast on the one hand was funny but on the other hand it cost me and I felt obliged to pay up. When I asked Kevin about this he just grinned and said "Well, they gave it to me".

You're Being Ridiculous!

It's fair to say that Kevin-says-no and Bailey were smitten with each other. Actually, Kevin could be quite rough with me sometimes but with Bailey he was soft as putty. He fed Bailey all his meals everyday for the duration of his time with me and I think Bailey was a good calming influence on him. The weekends we had together were a nice mixture of leisure and activity. I was able to be the pyjama slob that I often aspire to be on a Saturday or Sunday morning, sometimes both, and Kevin and I either entertained ourselves at home or with walks or trips to the park or beach. Kevin didn't think these things were for babies and nor did he find me obtuse.

I hope Kevin is okay. I often think of him as I do them all, but there was a vulnerability around this slightly cheeky little man that I hope can be dissipated with continued love and security.

You're Being Ridiculous!

Chapter 17
Pwsssh, ktcha

The next phone call came in but it came with time to prepare, and the information I was given suggested this might be another longer term placement. I was ready as ever and as prepared as is possible. Jamie was five and in his first year at primary school. The doorbell went, I still felt that slight sense of anxiety or anticipation when opening the door for the first time, I suspect I always will. You have no idea what they look like, of their personalities, nothing apart from the issues they may have or the reason for them being placed in foster care and that doesn't ever make for pleasant reading. So, I opened the door and in came Jamie in a not too dissimilar fashion to Owen and Neil. He burst through the front door all smiles and laughter. He rushed straight into the kitchen, desperate to meet Bailey who he had been told about and then, bored with him after only a few seconds, he raced into the sitting room. He didn't venture upstairs, out into the garden or up the apple tree but he very quickly ensconced himself in a box of toys and was happily chuntering away to himself as I sat with the social worker, Linda, who had brought him to me. Linda, unusually in my experience, wasn't in a hurry to get away and so we sat having a cup of tea while Jamie happily played and without any need or want for interaction. This in itself was a little strange to me that for over half an hour he hadn't needed to speak to either of us but, as it turned out, that had a lot to do with his history and circumstances. Linda left me to it and this gorgeous little scrap was soon to worm his way into my affections and vice versa but not without a few challenges along the way.

Given that he was five, Jamie was actually very young for his age in every developmental way. His speech wasn't good, comparable to a two year old I would say, but this would change very quickly. He was not doing particularly well in school although, as I have previously alluded to with other children, he loved school and the security that it provides. Not once did I ever have any problem in getting Jamie to school, and the longer he was with me the more he actually benefitted, eventually catching up with his classmates both in height and in ability. Jamie was cute, very, very cute and he knew it. He was full of I-love-yous from the word go and while you and I know this could not have been real in the beginning it definitely became real for both of us after several months - but I'll begin at the beginning.

Our first evening was fairly uneventful. My inner dictator was ready in the background but was not really required. Jamie had his tea, he had a bath, a story and he appeared as a happy bubbly little boy. He was sound asleep by seven o'clock in the evening, almost like a baby, out like a light and there was no sound from him until three o'clock in the morning and then the "few minor problems" began. You will know or have maybe guessed by now how much I love my sleep. I need it and can't function without it, becoming this person that even I dislike if I don't get a good eight or nine hours. Three o'clock in the morning is not the time for waking up and playing, as Jamie was soon to discover.

He hadn't got out of his bed but I could hear him chuntering away. I use the word chuntering as opposed to chattering as it wasn't words he was using, it was sounds. "Pwsssh, pwsssh, ktcha, ktcha" I wasn't sure what he was doing, thinking or playing, but it was three a.m. and I needed it to stop. I calmly, and yes, I am proud of myself for remaining calm, went into his room to see him. He beamed at me and it was hard to feel cross or to be firm but if you remember my motto from my rookie days, I needed to start as I meant to go on. I said "Jamie, do you need to go to the toilet?". He said he did and so we went through to the bathroom. He was seemingly wide awake now, not even a hint of drowsiness but I led him back to his bed, he climbed in and I tucked him in again. I said "Jamie, listen to me, it's the middle of the night and it's not time for us to be awake yet. You need to stay in your bed and try to go back to sleep, okay". He lay back, eyes wide open and gave me a look that I took to mean okay. I went back to my bed, still half asleep and hoped that we would both be able to drift off again. No chance!

It was probably two minutes later, albeit I was just on the edge of going off again, when I heard him "Pwsssh, pwsssh, ktcha, ktcha, gling, gling". The most nonsensical, annoying and utterly ridiculous sounds that you could ever imagine. What part of go back to sleep did he not understand? I tried to ignore it, but it was like a dripping tap or a clock that ticks too loudly and to me it was simply torture. With my head under the pillow for a further twenty minutes I could still hear him, "Whana, whana, whana, Pwsssh, ktcha, yonky, yonky".

Ridiculous, ridiculous, ridiculous! How am I supposed to get up tomorrow, or today, get him to school and do a day's work if I can't sleep? I decided to try again and calmly, yes calmly although falsely calm by now, I went through to his room, opened his door and said really softly "Jamie, you're not sleeping are you and you're not being quiet?" He looked at me and said something that sounded like he was asking if it was morning yet. I said "I'll tell you when it's the morning, I'll come in here and say good morning", I was slightly singing it in a fun sort of way combined with some stupid jazz hands to try to encourage him to sleep until the fun begins. He seemed to understand me and so I said in the same soft kind of fake voice "remember, no more talking or sounds now. I want you to try really hard to go back to sleep". He even exaggeratedly squeezed his eyes shut this time and I skipped off back to my bed almost excited that this may have worked.

I would say it was at least thirty seconds before "Pwsssh, pwsssh, ktcha, ktcha, gling, gling". Imagine any expletive you have ever heard and you can be sure that one or all of them were not far from the tip of my tongue. I sat on the edge of my bed, head in my hands, trying to work out how to handle this.

Realistically of course I knew that it was my problem and not his but I was so tired I was beginning to feel irrational. I'm not proud of feeling like this and in a very gentle voice I called out to him "Jamie you're not being quiet". I wondered if perhaps this would work this time but no, the pwsshh continued. I lay there, now wide awake in fury and I don't think I slept again that night and neither did he.

I went into his room at seven thirty in the morning, he was wide awake and seemingly had been for the past four and a half hours. I had my bright and breezy face on, I was dressed and ready for work and as promised I made his morning fun by saying good morning in a sing-song voice; I think I even used the ridiculous jazz hands.

Jamie and I had breakfast, he looked so cherubic, dressed in his school uniform and like butter wouldn't melt in his mouth. I was on about my third cup of coffee, wondering how on earth I was going to get through my day at work. Jamie ate a hearty breakfast and was just so excited about everything, but it was hard to actually understand what it was he was trying to say. I have to confess I was looking forward to getting him to school. I tried to subtly mention the night and how he really needed to be quiet and actually try to sleep or he would be tired at school or wouldn't grow taller but he just beamed at me with the most beautiful smile that I now know to mean; "Give it up Claire, I'm the cute one and I'm in charge here".

You're Being Ridiculous!

Chapter 18
Counting

The next few days, weeks and even months were hard. Sleep deprivation for me thankfully only lasted about two weeks before he realised that it was actually nice to have a good night's sleep. I know two weeks of no sleep to those of you who have had your own children is nothing, but remember, I chose not to have my own and perhaps somewhere in my subconscious this is because I know I wouldn't have survived the sleepless nights. Jamie and I had the same routines every single day and not once did I deviate from them. He very quickly started to transform into the clever little boy that he naturally is. It was in Jamie's nature to try to be very controlling with everything that he did or was asked to do, but with firm boundaries he soon relaxed, and in the knowledge that he was going to be looked after, fed and loved he became a totally different boy in a matter of months. Jamie was in fact a trooper. He was bold, he was brave and he was beautiful. He was with me for a few years and there are so many different tales to tell, none of which are as traumatic as that first day with Owen and Neil but are just as equally memorable for me. Bailey was a big part of family life and while it took Jamie time to realise he couldn't hit or hurt Bailey they eventually developed their own little bond. I'll do my best now to write of some of the most memorable things that Jamie was to say or do.

Probably one of my clearest memories from the very early days, and in line with the mental torture that he seemed to enjoy inflicting on me, was a trip that we took which involved a two hour car journey. Now, Jamie was very good in the car but this journey was so awful it's almost hard for me to write about without making me feel all hot and bothered again. He had just learnt to count to one hundred or so he thought. He had come such a long way from not being able to count even to five and so I should have been feeling super proud of him, and I was proud but only to a point.

We set off and within a mile from home it became apparent that counting was what Jamie wanted to do to pass the time. Fair enough, I was fine with this as I would always do anything to encourage his learning. So, he started at one, forgive me because I'm going to assume that you can count, and he carried on until he reached 25 and then it went like this....26, 27, 29, 28, 30......I stopped him nicely and said "Jamie, you got that a little bit the wrong way round, it should be 26, 27, 28, 29" - you know how it goes. So he began again from 1... but then the same thing happened again and so I reluctantly stopped him and said nicely "No Jamie you went a bit wrong again" and I explained again how it goes. He accepted help very happily and there were certainly no tears or tantrums at being corrected but after the fifth or sixth time of correcting and only ten miles away from home I let him carry on right the way to 50 with the 7, 9 & 8 in the wrong order.

It was really hurting my head, it was torture, and I tried to encourage another distraction by counting yellow cars or anything that I hoped might take a while for him to get to 20. Jamie was not wanting to do this and was not going to be swayed so on he went.

What was I to do? Keep on stopping him or just let him get on and do it wrong? He obviously had a mental block with it or he was intentionally trying to torture me and so I just decided to let him get on with it so that he could achieve his aim of reaching one hundred. He was quite delighted when he finally got there and I praised him for it, even though I felt I possibly should point out it still wasn't right. I shared in his jubilation in the hopes that this would be the end of it but no...Jamie wanted to do it all over again.

I had lost the will to live and couldn't concentrate on both the traffic and his counting so decided that our safety was more important than his ability to count. He started again at 1 and sure enough every 7, 9 & 8 was out of sequence right up to one hundred. There was nothing for it, the faster I went the sooner we would be there. The only problem with arriving was that I knew we would eventually have to depart again and so rather than relaxing for the day and enjoying time with my family I spent most of the day trying to get everyone to come up with at least 10 possible distractions for the journey home. I don't remember what these were but it's fair to say that none of them worked, and Jamie with his new found ability to count incorrectly started at one again the second we got in the car. I'm not a fast driver, I drive at the speed limit usually, but the speedometer was pushed on this occasion in my attempts to get him home as quickly as possible. I've often wondered whether a plea of torture would have stood up in a court of law had I been stopped for speeding; I suspect not but actually at the time, a night in the cells wouldn't have seemed a bad deal.

Jamie loved his bath time and bedtime stories and these occurred every night for the entire duration of his time with me. I recall reading him a bedtime story shortly before his sixth birthday; he was beside himself with excitement about it, and the book happened to be about a birthday, with a child blowing out candles on a cake. Jamie said to me "What are those?" pointing at the candles. I don't mind admitting I was a bit shocked, although by this point I knew Jamie and his background very well and so nothing really surprised me. I said "They're candles Jamie, they go on a birthday cake. Everyone sings Happy Birthday and then you blow them out". "I've never had candles before. Will I have candles on my cake for my birthday?" he said. "Yes you will Jamie, you will have six candles because that's how old you're going to be" I said, while also thinking to myself, I'm going to try to give you the best birthday you've ever had. You deserve it, little man.

You're Being Ridiculous!

Chapter 19
The Little Hole

When Jamie first came to live with me, he was only just out of training pants. Aside from one or two accidents he was dry the majority of the time but this next story shows his lack of knowledge in a certain area which caused me enormous embarrassment. I'm not sure embarrassment is the right word, as I'm not easily embarrassed and have no problems in discussing anything, but when something funny happens or is said by a small child, and you can't laugh about it because you either don't want to alert them to the fact that it's funny or you don't want to inhibit their willingness to talk about things, it makes you suppress your giggles and gives off an internal feeling of embarrassment.

Anyway, I was putting Jamie to bed one night and he was busy brushing his teeth and going to the toilet before bedtime. As he left the bathroom, I said to him "Jamie, I'm just going to the toilet before we read your story" and I shut the door. I did what I needed to do and came out of the bathroom and we sat and read his bed time story. When we had finished Jamie jumped out of bed saying that he needed to go to the toilet again and so while I thought this was a bedtime delaying tactic, I let him go.

He went into the bathroom and he came straight out again and said to me "Did you do a poo?" Slightly bemused, I said "No. Why, is there a poo in there?" thinking that perhaps one of us had been at some point and it maybe hadn't flushed but surely I would have just noticed? "No" he said "there's no poo but the seat was down and you said we only put the seat down if we're doing a poo". Oh no! "Well, girls have the seat down when they pee" I said. "Why?" he asked. "Because girls pee sitting down" I replied. "No they don't" he giggled. Oh my goodness, he really doesn't know this, how can he not know this? "Yes, Jamie, they do. Girls pee sitting down". He then asked "So how do they hold their penis?". Oh wow, this is going to be more complex than I had imagined. "Jamie, girls don't have a penis" I said. "Of course they do or how do they pee" he asked earnestly.

It occurs to me then that actually he really probably doesn't know. He's probably never even seen a girl or woman to notice the differences. If you think about it, it's one of those basic things that I guess happens or is noticed and talked about when children are considerably younger and if they miss out on this bit of enlightenment then they simply wouldn't know it. "Jamie, can we talk about this tomorrow morning" I try in vain. "No, Claire, I want to see your penis. If you don't have a penis then how do you pee?". Someone please help me! Phone, ring now so I can run for it...come on!!

Yet again, I know you are all reading this with your pre-prepared answers, and you probably think I'm a fool for not having the right response ready but this is what I was forced to say on the spur of the moment. "Well, Jamie, girls don't have a penis, they have a little hole that they pee out of". He was looking at me quizzically and I wondered if maybe this had been sufficient. "Can I see your little hole?" he said. There was no giggling or hilarity, he was being perfectly serious. "No Jamie" I said in a firm voice, "you can't because it's private and no one should ever see anyone else's privates". Was this going to be enough? He seemed thoughtful, but he then said "Please Claire, can I see your little hole, I've never seen one before?".

At this point I'm afraid I made the choice to get a little bit firmer and I went and found a doll that I had in the cupboard who didn't have a little hole but I thought this was as close an example to the real thing as I was going to be able to come up with. I showed him the doll and I said "Look Jamie, this is what girls look like, there's no penis and that is the difference between girls and boys". "Girls have babies, that's another difference" he said climbing into his bed. "I know I came out of my Mummy's tummy but you're my real Mummy aren't you?" My heart melted and I didn't have the strength to argue with him and I definitely wasn't wanting to begin a conversation on the hole that babies come from; it could wait for another day. I kissed him goodnight and as I was leaving the room he called out to me "Will you show me your little hole tomorrow?" I barked back at him "No Jamie, I will not, it's private and you will never see it and you can't call it a little hole, the real name is vagina". I know this isn't actually correct but I think it's what they're taught in school and in my experiences most men see it as being all encompassing. I hoped that my little factual outburst would stop this whole disastrous conversation. He repeated the word vagina several times as if checking he was saying it right and when satisfied that he had mastered it we said goodnight and I went downstairs to continue my own embarrassment with no further interruptions.

The next morning, I was woken up by Jamie gently poking his chubby finger in my face. He whispered softly to me saying my name with each poke "Claire...Claire... Claire...can I see your vagina now?" For heavens sake! I sat bolt upright "No Jamie, you can't. It's private and you have to stop asking, I will not change my mind, now go and get ready for school and I don't want to hear you ask again".

Now I had another problem, far bigger than I thought and I started to worry that I could have handled this so much better but I'm still not sure how? I was mortified that I was actually going to have to tell his teacher. I had visions of Jamie going into school and asking to see one of the girls' vagina or worse still, asking to see his teacher's. Oh my god, have I in that split second that I had to come up with an answer created some kind of future sex fiend? You may laugh, but there's nothing more embarrassing than being embarrassed all by yourself and with no one to share it with. I took Jamie to school and unfortunately his teacher wasn't about so I explained the whole sorry story to the classroom assistant. To my horror and further embarrassment she was laughing so hard she was actually crying. Fortunately for me, and the entire female population that Jamie has since encountered, I don't think he has ever mentioned the matter again or asked anyone to satisfy his curiosity. He seems to have accepted for the time being at least that it is private although further talk of a similar topic was discussed but in a different context. What is it with boys and their anatomy? I feel a bit perverse writing all of this but honestly they seem obsessed from the minute they're born to the day they die, and it seems to be never ending in my house.

Chapter 20
It's Furry

As time went on, Jamie was still growing and learning fast. We had several holidays, some abroad and some throughout the UK. Jamie was a game little boy, happy to enjoy new experiences and not shy in saying what he thought. There were difficulties along the way in terms of the planning of his future but he was a resilient boy and with support he dealt with these well. Jamie knew that I loved him but that he wouldn't be able to stay with me forever and I knew that the I love-you's that came from Jamie were very genuine now.

We took a fair few flights to various places during his time with me and I can remember one flight clearly; I had one large suitcase and this tough little boy was hauling another full-size suitcase that was bigger than he was and packed with Christmas presents. He pulled it right through the airport arrivals and outside into a pouring hail storm. With his hood up and his lips and nose blue from the cold, he battled on behind me to the car park where our lift awaited us. This is just a tiny example of the uncomplaining and by now uncomplicated child he was.

Both he and I had reached a point where everything was pretty perfect but the one liners or embarrassing questions kept on coming and yet again involving parts of the anatomy. I've often wondered if these are actually the most memorable things or are they the things that stick in my mind because they caused me embarrassment?

We were in a swimming pool changing room, I don't mind admitting I was afraid to take him swimming for a few weeks after the little hole incident but, whether forgotten or just stored to the back of his mind, he didn't mention it on this occasion. We were getting changed and he was all excited about going swimming, bouncing around the open changing rooms. Unfortunately there were several other ladies in there but he wasn't bothering them too much or at least they weren't tutting!

One of the ladies was drying herself and wasn't being particularly discreet. I'm not for a second saying she should have been discreet but Jamie, by now standing in his trunks on the benches staring, pointed at this lady and said loudly "Look Claire, it's furry!". Now, I'm not exactly one of these Brazilian styled women, I don't often have the time or inclination, and by now he had seen me changing many times at the pool, although I have to confess I was always really careful and had a towel around me pretty much all the time, but the titters, as opposed to tuts, in the changing room reverberated around the tiled walls and I wasn't quite sure what to say or do or whom to say it or do it to? I gave Jamie one of those stares that says "be quiet, be quiet now and don't speak again", and I gave the furry lady an apologetic smile at which she thankfully gave me a, "don't worry, I know what you're going through" smile back.

Jamie hopped and skipped, while I sidled out of the changing rooms, to the poolside where we went for our swim; these usually lasted for hours in an attempt to tire him out. It was great fun, as always, and we returned to the changing rooms to get dried and changed again.

There were as many ladies, albeit thankfully different ones, in the changing room when we got out and Jamie, not in the least shy, whipped off his trunks and went to do a poo, something he always seemed to need to do after we had been swimming. He would never close the door, even if asked to and would always sing at the top of his voice. He was actually quite tuneful and I had never to date succeeded in quietening him down, so I just let him sing, much to the amusement of my fellow swimmers.

I grabbed the opportunity to quickly dry and get dressed myself and by the time he was finished pooing and singing I was ready to get him dried and dressed. He was naked, with not a care in the world; I sometimes wonder if I should have tried to teach him to be a bit more coy but actually he learnt this himself the older he got. I was naïvely thinking everything was going to plan and this would be easy, when he

191

decided that now was the time to discuss breasts. "That lady has big ones" he whispered to me, in a tone that was said for affect and didn't resemble a whisper at all. "Shh," I said nicely but also giving him that look again that says. "don't speak". "I know what they are for" he said, obviously feeling knowledgeable, "they're for feeding a baby, aren't they?" "Yes, Jamie, that's right. Now lets get you dry" I said to try to stop this conversation. It worked, or so I had thought, until he then said, definitely not in a whisper, "and babies come from girls' tummies don't they?". "Yes, Jamie, that's right they do" I confirmed, not wanting to go down any little hole route again. I could absolutely tell by his face, not to mention his still dripping wet, goose pimply body that he was refusing to allow me to dry until he had resolved the whirring cogs in his head, that this was not over. "Come here" I said " I need to get you dry or you'll start to get cold". I wrapped him in a towel and had him sat on my knee in a vice like grip and I inanely babbled on, talking excitedly about the swimming we had just done and that perhaps when we got home he could sit and watch a film, anything to distract him and change his course of thought. No luck!

He was dried but wriggled out of my clasp and stood right in front of me and said, definitely not in a whisper "How does a daddy get his seeds from here" as he stood holding his own penis "into a mummy's tummy?" I don't believe it! I was grimacing while thinking to myself, why Jamie? Why now and why here? How do you even know about seeds? Did he learn this in school, because he's never mentioned seeds before? All of a sudden I realised that what I had called embarrassment in the past with various dildo or little hole questions had not been actual embarrassment; this was embarrassment and there was an audience.

Now, I know you are sitting comfortably knowing exactly what you would say and well, good for you, but I was caught out again and with no time to think, so I said "That's a good question Jamie". I only said that to buy me a bit more time and it didn't really help. Aware of the titters and the smothered giggles surrounding us and the variety of females literally shaking with suppressed laughter but eagerly awaiting my response I said " Come on, we need to get you dressed and get home. Bailey will be wanting his tea so I'll tell you later". Had this worked? Had it heck! Jamie, still standing there with no clothes on, still holding his willy, declared very knowledgeably "I think I know" he said earnestly, "the seeds come out of here", well at least he had pointed to the correct little hole for that fact "and they go into the daddy's hand and he then gives it to the mummy to eat and that's how the baby gets into her tummy!". Ohhhh Help! I think that I actually blushed and I never blush. Two older ladies, I should think in their seventies, actually had to leave the room and went back round the corner to the showers, their hands clasped over their mouths, bodies convulsing with suppressed laughter. Several other ladies were looking at me expectantly with a glint in their eye suggesting "What are you going to reply to that then? Come on, we're waiting!" Some of the younger girls in the room just looked at him in horror and disgust that this could even have entered his head. I just looked at him with no expression at all. I didn't know what to express or what to do? So, I probably did completely the wrong thing but it was the only thing that would give us any potential speed in vacating the building and I said "I suspect you're probably right Jamie, perhaps not quite correct but near enough". He beamed at me as he thought he was right and in that moment and with no further questions or statements I was happy to let him think he was right. I got him dressed and the older tittering ladies eventually reappeared around the corner, mouthing sorry to me, I presume they were meaning sorry for the stifled laughter to which I mouthed back – I'm sorry too!

Chapter 21

Love, Happiness and Laughter

Jamie continued to flourish and grow and he really was, and I hope still is, the most remarkable boy. He does now know a little more about babies and where they come from, and he is the most loving, caring compassionate boy so I feel quite comfortable and confident that one day he may become the best husband to some lucky girl and the best dad too. He left my care, and heart breaking as this was, he left with a confidence and resilience that will help to get him through any further trials or tribulations. I hope he will always carry with him some little pieces of me, the good pieces preferably, the ability to love unconditionally, to laugh until you cry and to just cry whenever you feel the need.

On that note, I will end with this last final and very meaningful moment that was said just a few days before Jamie left my care.

Jamie and I are watching E.T, it is his second or even third time of watching it, and so he is quite used to seeing me cry at various points throughout it. I can't help it, even though I know the film inside out it always makes me well up. I'm a pretty soft and mushy person really. Anyway, we are sitting together watching this film, a treat for him and forming part of my lazy weekend, and it get's to the bit at the end where Elliot and E.T are saying good bye. I've got silent tears rolling down my cheeks and Jamie is looking at me, completely comfortable and confident in his own skin by now, like the majority of men do when they see a woman crying. The kind of look that is saying, oh no, not the waterworks again, what am I to do?

The film finished, we laughed at me getting upset over E.T and I dried my tears while also thinking ahead about what I was going to make for our tea. Without warning and just as I was about to get up, Jamie came and sat on my knee with a little solemn face and said to me his most poignant one liner. "Claire" he said, looking me straight in the eyes and pointing his little finger to my forehead "I will always be right here". Well, I had to suppress every emotion and thought I was feeling so as not to actually burst into tears. This little man, the current love of my life, was trying to tell me in the words of E.T that he would always be in my head. In my best E.T voice, so as to try to lighten the mood, I repeated this action, pointing my finger to his forehead and said "and Jamie, I will always be right here too". We had a cuddle, both a little teary eyed as we knew he would be leaving me soon, and I then went away to the kitchen to start the tea, leaving Jamie happily playing in the sitting room. I stood at the kitchen sink for a few minutes where I was able to let the tears out properly.

I think of all my boys regularly but not a day passes when I don't think of Owen, Neil and Jamie because they were with me for so long. I love them with all of my heart and will always love them as if they were my own. They have given me more love, happiness, laughter and fulfilment than I could ever have imagined when embarking on this life as a foster carer and I can only hope that maybe one day they will come back to tell me how they are doing.

I do wonder now though if perhaps the next phone call may be for a girl?

Acknowledgements

A special thank you to those family and friends who have supported and encouraged me to publish this little book. I must thank my Dad, aged 82, for being chief copy-editor, proof reader and general 'go to' person; exasperated with my lack of grammar and style of writing, I hope he makes it to 83! Thanks also to my Mum for pestering me to write down these memories, I'm not sure this book is what you had in mind but it's done now! Huge thanks to Lyndsay for putting the idea of writing a book into my head. A big thank you to Claire and Karen, my oldest and wisest friends, who gave me the confidence to pursue this and last, but by no means least, to Jo for your continued friendship and support; and not least your new-found proof reading skills. There are so many others to mention, you know who you are. Thank you all!